ATLANTIC PAPER № 65

Macroeconomic Diplomacy in the 1980s:

ATLANTIC PAPER Nº 65

Macroeconomic Diplomacy in the 1980s

Domestic Politics and International Conflict among the United States, Japan, and Europe

C. Randall Henning

CROOM HELM
London · New York · Sydney
for THE ATLANTIC INSTITUTE FOR INTERNATIONAL AFFAIRS

© 1987 The Atlantic Institute for International Affairs
Croom Helm Ltd, Provident House, Burrell Row,
Beckenham, Kent BR3 1AT
Croom Helm Australia, 44-50 Waterloo Road,
North Ryde, 2113, New South Wales

Published in the USA by
Croom Helm
in association with Methuen, Inc.
29 West 35th Street
New York, NY 10001

British Library Cataloguing in Publication Data

Henning, C. Randall
    Macroeconomic diplomacy in the 1980s:
    domestic politics and international
    conflict among the United States,
    Japan and Europe. — (Atlantic
    paper: no. 65).
    1. Economic policy   2. Macroeconomics
    I. Title II. Atlantic Institute for
    International Affairs III. Series
    339   HD87
    ISBN 0-7099-3794-6

Library of Congress Cataloging in Publication Data

ISBN 0-7099-3794-6

Printed and bound in Great Britain by
Biddles Ltd, Guildford and King's Lynn

Contents

The Author

C. Randall Henning is a Research Associate at the Institute for International Economics in Washington, D.C., where he writes on topics in international political economy. He earned his PhD degree at The Fletcher School of Law and Diplomacy, Tufts University, with a thesis on the politics of macroeconomic policy conflict and coordination. He has recently co-authored a publication on the Bonn Summit of 1978.

Acknowledgements

Many people have been helpful to me in the course of writing this paper. Officials concerned with economic policy in Washington, D.C. and other capitals contributed by granting off-the-record interviews. The paper has benefited from informal discussions with colleagues at the Institute for International Economics. As parts of my PhD dissertation have been incorporated here, I am grateful for the advice received on that project from Benjamin J. Cohen and Robert O. Keohane, as well as discussion with Robert D. Putnam. The Atlantic Institute supplied valuable logistical support for which I am also grateful. Benjamin Cohen, John Williamson and Mario Kakabadse offered their comments, Linda Giacchino gave research assistance, and Renae Sledge ably helped me with the manuscript. I alone am responsible for the errors and omissions.

C. Randall Henning

Foreword

Given the high degree of financial interdependence that exists today, it is desirable that countries design and implement their domestic economic policies with a view to maintaining a mutually beneficial system of international capital flows. The experience of floating exchange rates since the collapse of the Bretton Woods system has been disappointing and has led to a renewed desire for more closely managed exchange rates and for more consciously coordinated economic policies.

Yet there are serious doubts that national goals and policies can be harmonized to a sufficient degree to guarantee a viable international system. Economic cooperation between the United States, Europe and Japan encounters serious problems because countries differ in their institutional structures, policy objectives and political constraints. Experience to date suggests that there is little common understanding of the way national economies function. Consequently, there is only limited agreement on the benefits which may arise from policy coordination and even on what the actual policies should be.

In this timely and valuable study Dr Randall Henning offers a thoughtful and thorough analysis of the issues at stake in attempting to reconcile the conflict between the need for international macroeconomic stability and the desire for national political autonomy. Dr Henning also makes an important contribution to the policy discussion on the desirability and feasibility of instituting more systematic macroeconomic and monetary cooperation on a continuing basis as an alternative to the crisis management which has characterized international economic developments over the past fifteen years.

Andrew J. Pierre

Introduction

The advanced industrial democracies will confront unprecedented adjustments in their economic relations during the
remainder of this decade. The imbalances among these countries in trade and capital flows are simply too large to be
sustained at 1986 levels. What remains to be seen is whether the
advanced market economies remain healthy throughout the
process of adjustment. This depends, in turn, on whether adjustment is achieved through economic cooperation or rivalry. The
coordination of macroeconomic policies is a fundamental
element in a cooperative solution to these problems. However,
unless the major governments use the finance ministers of
the Group of Five (composed of France, Germany, Japan,
the United Kingdom and the United States), seven-power
economic summit meetings, and international organizations,
such as the International Monetary Fund, to organize coordination more successfully than during the early and mid-1980s,
they may well fail to reach the needed level of cooperation.
Hanging in the balance between successful coordination and
failure may be the prosperity of the advanced market countries,
the solvency of indebted developing countries, and, ultimately,
the integration of the world economy.

Conflicts over the responsibility for undertaking international
adjustment have persistently confounded the United States,
Japan, and Europe in their postwar economic relations. Unable,
in the early 1970s, to agree on how adjustment obligations
should be divided among them, these countries had to disband
the Bretton Woods system of fixed exchange rates. Flexible
exchange rates, however, have not eliminated the need for
collective decision-making on macroeconomic performance and

the distribution of adjustment burdens. Consequently, governments have wavered between contentment with flexible rates and attempts at greater macroeconomic coordination in order to dampen fluctuations in exchange rates. On balance, the post-Bretton Woods period has been a mix of little coordination and much exchange rate instability.

This legacy has been inherited in the 1980s. Dominated by conflict, macroeconomic diplomacy has, so far, had two distinct phases. Throughout the period 1981–83, the Europeans and Japanese were bitterly critical of American fiscal and monetary policy, which, they argued, caused unnecessarily high interest rates. The first Reagan administration steadfastly refused to modify its fiscal strategy to accommodate foreign complaints. During the years 1984–86, the Reagan administration pursued an aggressive international reflation strategy, while the Europeans and Japanese reacted defensively, trying to deflect American pressure for policy change, but continuing to complain about the large U.S. budget deficits. While greater cooperation has recently been achieved on exchange rates, and to some extent on monetary policy, meaningful cooperation on fiscal policy remains inchoate. Insufficient coordination has left the world economy exposed to great risks.

To understand why it is so difficult for countries to arrive at mutually beneficial macroeconomic agreements, it is essential to explore how governments influence the macroeconomic policy decisions of others, and how international controversies affect domestic debates and vice versa. This study, in sections one and two, reviews current thinking on the role of state power and domestic politics in macroeconomic conflict and coordination, and sketches the economic background. It then traces, in chapters three and four, the evolution of macroeconomic and monetary relations among the advanced market countries during the disputes over interest rates and reflation. This history suggests, in the fifth section, that American macroeconomic power has played an essential role in the conflict in the 1980s, but that power alone has been, and probably will continue to be, an insufficient basis on which to build hopes for trilateral coordination with Germany and Japan. Domestic politics are fundamental in determining whether states can reach ad hoc and intertemporal bargains on international adjustment and its attendant political costs. Domestic politics and policy-making processes also determine whether states learn from conflict and policy mistakes. Therefore, the task for architects of an international macroeconomic regime is not to isolate international deliberations from domestic politics, but to bridge the two constructively — this is discussed in the last section of the paper.

The definitions of key terms used here are conventional. Both monetary and fiscal policy comprise *macroeconomic policy*. *Fiscal policy* refers to taxes, government spending, and the budget deficit. *Monetary policy* is principally composed of interest rate and money supply growth policies. *International monetary policy* refers to exchange rate policy and policies regarding international finance and liquidity. Macroeconomic policies are *discordant* or *conflicting* when the policies of one state hinder or constrain the policies of other states from reaching potential macroeconomic performance. *Coordination* is the reduction of discord and increase in harmony among national policies. It is a process by which the policies of each state are adjusted to reduce the adverse consequences, or reinforce the positive effects, as the participants define them, for the policies of other states. When that process reduces discord through mutual adjustment, the outcome is *cooperation*.[1] It is important to note that the degree of coordination of policies is a separate question from their content or merit. Coordinated policies may be either deflationary or reflationary, convergent or divergent, economically wise or flawed. However, while policies may be coordinated to the detriment of national economic interests, it is also true that coordination is often necessary for welfare maximization.

I
State Power and
Domestic Politics

Macroeconomic performance is at the center of governments' national objectives, and consequently domestic political imperatives necessarily complicate international coordination. In macroeconomic and international monetary affairs (perhaps more than in any other issue area) Stanley Hoffmann's observation that interdependence enhances the importance of domestic factors in international politics holds true.[2] German Finance Minister Gerhard Stoltenberg's recent statements are illustrative. 'The limit of expanded cooperation lies in the fact that we are democracies and we need to secure electoral majorities at home,' he has said, in response to foreign pleas that Germany stimulate domestic demand.[3] No astute observer would argue that domestic politics are not relevant to macroeconomic diplomacy.

Having said this, however, two additional points must be made. First, domestic politics need not always inhibit international coordination. The imperative of seeking constituency support for economic policy can, under certain circumstances, nudge governments *toward* cooperative agreements. Second, the international system can dominate domestic politics at times. When the constraints imposed by the system are strong, domestic political actors may have no other recourse but to adapt their position on economic issues to their international environment — in a fashion analogous to the internal restructuring of a business firm in response to the discipline of the marketplace. Thus, in certain circumstances, domestic political resistance to adjustment may be overwhelmed by international politics. The distribution of power among states — a fundamental attribute of the system — is, thus, at least potentially as important as domestic politics as an explanation of coordination success or failure and should be considered.

How domestic politics may work in favor of international coordination is illustrated by the Bonn economic summit of 1978. This summit was the most outstanding example of macroeconomic policy coordination since the breakdown of the Bretton Woods monetary regime.[4] The agreement concluded by the heads of government of the Group of Seven (the Group of Five with Canada and Italy) had as its core an exchange wherein the United States agreed to decontrol domestic oil prices, Germany offered a domestic fiscal stimulus, and the others also accepted trade and macroeconomic obligations. It has been argued that this accord shows that unanimity among important domestic political actors is not a necessary condition for international cooperation, and that, under certain circumstances, domestic discord may actually facilitate cooperation. Agreement was possible at Bonn only because a powerful minority within each key government actually favored, on domestic grounds, the policy being demanded internationally. These minority factions used the summit process to get their head of government to accede to their position. 'In the end, each leader believed that what he was doing was in his nation's interest and his own, even though not all his aides agreed. Yet without the summit he probably would not (or could not) have changed policies so easily. In that sense, the Bonn deal successfully meshed domestic and international pressures.'[5]

As governments are frequently internally divided over the proper course of macroeconomic policy, current policy represents the resultant vector, so to speak, of the pushing and hauling of competing coalitions, one dominant, one weaker. The effect of the summits is to strengthen the ability of national leaders to guide domestic policy-making in the direction of international cooperation; in the words of a former summit aide, 'providing a bare majority for the previously stymied actions of a strong minority.'[6] Putnam and Bayne, in their leading study of the Group of Seven (G-7) summits, list a number of issues considered at the meetings where international pressure found domestic 'resonance,' and vice versa, culminating in agreements.[7]

Domestic politics are not entirely dominant in macroeconomic diplomacy, however. The exercise of power by some states, interpreted for analytical purposes to be unitary, rational actors, is often important in macroeconomic conflict and in inducing some countries to undertake policy adjustments. Even though the United States did not have the ability or willingness to reconstruct a strong international monetary regime in the 1970s, it retains the ability to significantly alter the opportunity costs to others of maintaining a fixed policy course. The United States can influence governments to adopt policy changes that they otherwise would not adopt, and to deflect others' attempts to change U.S. policies. The United States has, in other words, macroeconomic power. Through its relative size and closure, the dominance of its currency, the international substitutability of its financial assets, the United States can alter the incentives and disincentives for policy change facing other governments. American insulation from the effects of large swings in the exchange rate, relative to its economic partners, is a particularly important source of leverage.[8]

An important subschool of international political economy contends that hegemonic power, the guarantor against free riding and the enforcer of agreements, is essential to international cooperation.[9] When the United States conflicts with other countries over the proper level of world aggregate demand, or the distribution of demand among the Group of Five (G-5), for example, macroeconomic and declaratory policies promoting dollar depreciation provide incentives to foreign governments to conform to American wishes. In response to downward pressure on the dollar, foreign central banks may choose to intervene in the foreign exchange market. In this case, foreign demand is stimulated by an increase in foreign money supply and reduction in interest rates, to the extent that intervention is unsterilized. If foreign governments choose to allow their currencies to appreciate against the dollar, other economic changes will tend to nudge them toward adjustment. Currency appreciation will reduce exports and, thus, growth prospects at the same time as it retards domestic price increases. By providing an incentive and removing a constraint to the stimulation of foreign demand, the United States alters the opportunity costs of resistance to adjustment on the part of other governments. If American officials were more concerned about inflation than growth, they could apply pressure on foreign governments to institute deflationary policies through an appreciation of the dollar.

Three additional observations are in order. First, the United

States has no monopoly over this kind of influence. Other countries influence the cost-benefit calculations of their neighbors' policies, particularly Germany in the European Community. Second, the United States is not invulnerable to adverse effects of dollar depreciation or appreciation on its own rates of inflation and growth. But, because it has a large and, arguably, relatively autonomous economy, the United States is less susceptible to these effects than are its economic partners. That asymmetry is fundamental. Third, the strength of these changes in opportunity costs in comparison to other forces, such as the positions of key domestic political actors, is not self-evident. We must examine actual cases of conflict to determine the relative importance of state power.[10]

Analysts of international cooperation relying on game theory share with power-structure theorists the assumption that states are unitary, rational actors, and that domestic politics have relatively little value in explaining international cooperation. Economists using game theory have asked whether each country, pursuing its own macroeconomic interests, will adopt policies which are optimal from the collective standpoint.[11] Under the assumptions of both fixed and flexible exchange rates, the answer generally has been that, in fact, there is no invisible macroeconomic 'guiding hand.' In the international macroeconomic policy game, countries often settle into suboptimal equilibria, where one state can be made better off without making another worse off, for example, through the trading of a fiscal expansion in one country for the same in another. These economists' work convincingly establishes the normative case for international macroeconomic coordination.[12] It has been left to international political economists, however, to investigate how state power and international institutions condition cooperation.[13]

The recent history of macroeconomic diplomacy sheds light on the relative importance of state power and domestic politics in determining conflict and its outcome. Before proceeding to the story of international negotiations and domestic policy making, it is necessary to review the economic conditions faced by the major actors.

4

II
The Economic Backdrop to Diplomacy

International conflict over macroeconomic policy in the 1980s was played out against the backdrop of dramatic and continuing changes in the world economy. Led by the American economy, the advanced countries slipped into the deepest recession in decades between 1980 and 1982. The recession produced an international financial crisis as many developing countries became unable to service their high levels of external debt. (In several indebted developing countries, real per capita income has not yet recovered to levels reached in the early 1970s). The world economy rebounded in 1983, led once again by the American economy. The Reagan administration seemed to embark, in the words of one observer, on a full-scale 'experiment in global Keynesianism.'[14] The consequences for exchange rates, trade and current account balances, international capital flows, national net creditor and debtor positions were far reaching.

At the advent of the 1980s, the advanced industrial democracies were jolted by the second oil shock. Inflation in the member countries of the Organization for Economic Cooperation and Development (OECD) reached 9.5 percent in 1980, its postwar peak.[15] Governments were nearly unanimous in giving first priority to the fight against inflation.[16] The United States, Japan, the United Kingdom, Germany and France each invoked contractionary monetary measures. Although national budgets suffered some cyclical deterioration, important efforts were made to reduce structural budget deficits in nearly all of the G-5 countries in 1980–81.

These policies induced the most severe recession since the 1930s in the United States, and since World War II in Europe.

TABLE 1:
INFLATION, GROUP OF FIVE, 1980–86

	1980	1981	1982	1983	1984	1985	1986[a]
United States	9.1	9.6	6.5	3.8	3.9	3.4	2.8
Japan	3.8	3.2	1.9	0.8	1.3	1.7	1.8
Germany	4.8	4.0	4.4	3.2	1.6	2.2	2.8
France	12.2	11.9	12.6	9.5	7.2	5.8	4.5
United Kingdom	19.9	11.7	7.3	5.1	3.9	6.1	3.8

Source: IMF, *World Economic Outlook* (October 1986), 46.
a. Estimate

In 1982, the OECD economies contracted 0.7 percent, and area unemployment increased to 8.1 from 5.7 percent in 1980. At this cost, a reduction in the rate of inflation to 7.8 percent was achieved.[17] During 1981 and 1982, the mix of tight monetary policy and loosening fiscal policy in the United States became a major international issue. As the recession deepened, the Europeans and Japanese tended to shift their own policy mixes in the opposite direction, restraining spending while trying to ease monetary policy.[18] Their monetary loosening was restricted, however, by high American interest rates.

The American economy began to recover in the first half of 1983, in response to the growing federal budget deficit and monetary expansion initiated in mid-1982. It registered an impressive 6.6 percent gain in 1984 and continued to improve in 1985, pulling the European and Japanese economies with it.

TABLE 2:
UNEMPLOYMENT, GROUP OF FIVE, 1980–86

	1980	1981	1982	1983	1984	1985	1986[a]
United States	7.2	7.6	9.7	9.6	7.5	7.2	6.9
Japan	2.0	2.2	2.4	2.6	2.7	2.6	2.8
Germany	3.4	4.9	6.8	8.2	8.1	8.2	7.9
France	6.6	7.7	8.4	8.6	10.0	10.4	10.7
United Kingdom	6.5	10.1	11.5	11.9	12.4	11.3	11.6

Source: IMF, *World Economic Outlook* (October 1986), 41.
a. Estimate

6

By 1985, average OECD Gross National Product (GNP) was more than 10 percent above the 1982 trough, and inflation had progressively declined to 4.5 percent for the area. However, as European and Japanese demand did not accelerate as fast as American demand, the international transmission of the recovery was only partial. The rate of unemployment remained at postwar levels in Europe, with no foreseeable prospect of a substantial decline.

By 1986, American fiscal policy had provided as much stimulus as it could. While monetary policy had been loosened, both potential inflation and current account financing needed further constrained unilateral easing. The U.S. recovery had come and the limits to American demand expansion had been reached. American growth would have to rely increasingly on improvements in the trade balance. European growth, however, had recovered only modestly and was flagging. While domestic demand managed to outpace the fall-off in net exports which resulted from the appreciation of the mark and yen, German and Japanese 1987 growth prospects remain uncertain despite confident forecasts by both governments.

Both the European and Japanese recoveries relied heavily on American demand to boost their exports. During 1980–85, Japanese domestic demand growth equalled American demand growth at an average annual rate of 2.5 percent. However, real GNP growth in Japan was 4.0 percent as compared to 1.9 percent in the United States during the same period (see Table 3). The external sector was responsible for more than a third of Japanese income gains during the 1980s, while it acted as a drag on American growth. Foreign demand, from Europe and the rest of the world, as well as the United States, contributed to an even larger proportion of West German growth. Real GNP in West Germany rose at an average rate of 1.2 percent during 1980–85, while domestic demand increased at a mere 0.3 percent, providing only one-quarter of the income gains.[19] As American demand buoyed the advanced economies, it also made a comparatively large contribution to the servicing of Third World debt through imports.[20] The large American current account deficits, which increased during the 1980s and which encouraged growth abroad, reached unprecedented levels for the postwar period, mirrored by record current account surpluses for Germany and Japan (see Table 4).

These payments imbalances coincided with dramatic changes

TABLE 3:
REAL GNP AND DOMESTIC DEMAND, GROUP OF FIVE AND EUROPE 1980–86

	1980	1981	1982	1983	1984	1985	1986ᵃ	Average 1980–85	Average 1983–85
United States									
GNP	−0.2	1.9	−2.5	3.5	6.5	2.2	2.7	1.9	4.1
Domestic demand	−1.8	2.2	−1.9	5.0	8.5	2.8	3.4	2.5	5.4
Japan									
GNP	4.3	3.7	3.1	3.2	5.1	4.6	2.6	4.0	4.3
Domestic demand	0.8	2.1	2.8	1.8	3.8	3.7	4.2	2.5	3.1
Germany									
GNP	1.5	0.0	−1.0	1.5	3.0	2.4	3.0	1.2	2.3
Domestic demand	1.0	−2.7	−2.0	2.0	2.0	1.4	4.2	0.3	1.8
France									
GNP	1.1	0.5	1.8	0.7	1.6	1.1	2.2	1.1	1.1
Domestic demand	2.1	−0.5	4.1	−0.4	0.6	1.6	3.3	1.3	0.6
United Kingdom									
GNP	−2.5	−1.5	1.8	3.3	2.5	3.3	2.4	1.2	3.0
Domestic demand	−3.3	−1.8	2.4	4.3	2.3	2.7	3.3	1.1	3.1
Europe									
GNP	1.4	−0.1	0.5	1.5	2.4	2.3	2.6	1.3	2.1
Domestic demand	1.6	−2.0	0.8	1.1	1.9	2.1	3.6	0.9	1.7

Source: IMF, *World Economic Outlook* (October 1986), 180.
a. Estimate

TABLE 4:
THE BALANCE OF PAYMENTS, 1977–86: INTERNATIONAL COMPARISON (BILLIONS OF DOLLARS)

	1977	1978	1979	1980	1981	1982	1983	1984	1985	1986[a]
United States										
Trade Account	−31.1	−34.2	−29.5	−25.3	−27.9	−36.3	−60.6	−114.1	−124.3	−144.3
Current Account	−15.3	−13.9	−0.8	3.7	4.5	−8.1	−40.8	−107.4	−117.7	−138.0
Japan										
Trade Account	17.3	24.6	1.8	2.1	20.0	18.0	31.5	44.2	56.0	86.3
Current Account	10.9	16.5	−8.8	−10.7	4.8	6.9	20.8	35.0	49.3	81.8
Germany										
Trade Account	19.3	25.5	17.8	10.4	17.9	26.3	21.8	22.9	28.9	53.5
Current Account	3.7	8.8	−5.5	−16.4	−7.3	3.3	3.9	7.0	13.2	32.5
France										
Trade Account	−2.8	0.7	−2.1	−13.0	−10.1	−15.5	−8.2	−4.1	−5.4	−2.7
Current Account	−3.3	7.0	5.2	−4.2	−4.7	−12.0	−4.4	−0.7	−0.2	3.8
United Kingdom										
Trade Account	−3.0	−2.3	−7.2	2.7	6.0	3.7	−1.3	−5.8	−2.7	−11.8
Current Account	0.5	2.0	−3.9	7.5	12.1	9.5	4.8	2.1	4.6	−0.3

Source: OECD, *Economic Outlook* 22-40 (December 1977–December 1986), and OECD *Economic Survey*, selected issues.
Note: The current account is the sum of the trade balance, net services and private and official transfers.
a. Estimate

in the net savings and investment positions of these countries. The U.S. federal budget deficit and resurgent private investment accompanying the recovery raised the demand for savings in the United States, while fiscal contraction and lower growth of domestic demand in Japan and Germany, in particular, freed savings for foreign (American) use. As a consequence, capital flowed into the United States from abroad, in response initially to interest rate differentials which favored dollar-denominated financial assets. During 1980–82, the United States experienced little capital inflow on a net basis; Germany and Japan were in near balance on the capital account as well. By 1985, however, U.S. capital inflow amounted to 3.0 percent of GNP, while Japan and Germany exported capital in amounts equivalent to 3.1 and 2.0 percent of GNP, respectively, much of it going directly to the United States.[21]

These changes in the savings-investment balances were the product of opposing fiscal policy shifts in the United States compared to those in other OECD countries. Outside the United States policy shifts were continuously restrictive: for Germany, the United Kingdom, and Japan, taken as a group, the restrictive fiscal shift totaled 4 percent of GNP over that six-year period. In marked contrast, between 1981 and 1985, the expansionary shift of U.S. fiscal policy amounted to more than 3 percent of GNP. The United States' federal budget deficit rose from $78.9 billion in 1981 to $207 billion in 1983, and to $212 billion in 1985.[22]

Monetary policy in the United States was very tight from the end of 1979 through mid-1982. Nominal interest rates were both high and very volatile. Real short-term rates hit the 10 percent mark on three separate occasions during the period. The monetary policies of the Europeans and Japanese tended to follow the American lead. Nonetheless, the differential in long-term real rates between the American and German markets, for example, floated in the 2–4 percent range during 1982–85, as did the American-Japanese differential during 1983–85.[23]

American Debt

Responding initially to interest rate differentials, capital flowed into the United States in unprecedented quantities, reaching $123.6 billion in 1985. The regional sourcing of private sector

10

capital inflows was about evenly divided among Japan, Western Europe and the developing countries in that year.[24] Foreign savings became crucial to the U.S. recovery, financing 45 percent of U.S. net investment in early 1985.[25] Capital inflows spared the American economy from the interest rate increases that would otherwise have resulted from the burgeoning budget deficits. Instead of crowding out investment only in the United States, the budget deficit crowded out investment in the rest of the world as well.[26] Whether this is an appropriate international allocation of capital depends on how it has been invested in the United States in comparison to alternative uses, and remains an unresolved issue.

In 1983, the dollar averaged 33 percent above its value in 1980 in nominal terms — a value it subsequently exceeded, and did not return to until early 1986.[27] Williamson has estimated that at rates prevailing in late 1984 — from which the dollar appreciated in early 1985 — the mark needed to appreciate 50 percent and the yen 24 percent to reach their fundamental equilibrium rates.[28] These currency misalignments were the most important cause of the subsequent current account imbalances among the G-5 countries.[29]

A lasting result of this massive redistribution of capital among the advanced market economies has been a fundamental change in national net foreign asset positions. The United States became a net debtor in mid-1985 for the first time since World War I.[30] In 1986 it became the world's largest debtor, accumulating net foreign debt equal to approximately 6 percent of GNP by the end of the year. At exchange rates prevailing in early 1987, even optimistic projections forecast that the United States' net debtor position will stabililize, at no less than $500 billion in 1990. This debt would amount to roughly 10 percent of U.S. GNP at that time. Correspondingly, Japan has become the world's largest creditor nation, with a large share of its capital placed in the United States. The changed international financial status of the United States and Japan has fundamental and long-lasting implications for their bilateral relationship, as well as for the international monetary and financial system.[31]

These economic developments, driven largely by policy, became the object of hard-fought disputes among governments. With high unemployment during the 1980–82 recession, the United States, Europe and Japan confronted the problem of how to stimulate their economies. Europe and Japan relied heavily on positive changes in the current account; the transfer of savings abroad fits neatly into this strategy. Not all countries could pursue this strategy simultaneously, however. As Marina Whitman has observed, when foreign sources of demand are preferred, problems of world recovery are zero sum games.[32] As long as the United States was willing to bolster world demand, there was no conflict. But once reflationary American policies had run their course, the G-5 faced a classic reflationary dilemma of collective action.[33]

III
The Interest Rate
Controversy of 1981–83

In 1980, the United States, Europe and Japan were unified in giving top priority to reducing inflation. However, the recession which had been induced by deflationary policies undermined the inflation-fighting consensus within the OECD by mid-1981.[34] In the same year, the Reagan administration and Mitterrand government were inaugurated, each pledged to fundamentally different policy objectives. Domestic political developments thus hastened the breakdown of the fragile anti-inflation consensus.

Conflicting Policy Mixes

The incoming Reagan administration adopted a fiscal strategy that called for tax reductions *before* equivalent spending cuts were identified and passed by Congress. The most extreme 'supply-siders' in Washington believed that these tax cuts would be self-financing; others thought that even if supply-side economics did not live up to its claims, resulting deficits would put pressure on Congress to reduce domestic spending.[35] Meanwhile, the Reagan economic program also strongly endorsed a reduced money supply growth policy at the Federal Reserve (Fed). This was exactly the opposite approach to that taken by conservative governments abroad, which were determined that significant tax cuts would be enjoyed only *after* spending was reduced. They also sought to reduce unemployment, to the extent that inflation and foreign exchange pressures allowed, through more expansionary monetary policy.

Japan managed to avoid the recession during the early 1980s, although growth declined far below the levels to which the Japanese had become accustomed. The government became preoccupied with the size of the national debt which grew to nearly 60 percent of GNP in 1982, owing to continuously large budget deficits since the mid-1970s. Interest payments on the debt grew to roughly one-eighth of current expenditures. Prime Minister Suzuki pledged not to solve the deficit problem by raising taxes, however. Rather, at the insistence of the business community, he sought to reduce expenditures through a program of 'administrative reform.' So important was this program to the Prime Minister that he declared himself to be 'staking his political life' on its success.[36] Monetary policy, therefore, carried the main burden of stimulating domestic demand to offset the export slow down, as it had customarily done during the postwar period. Although the Japanese were more successful than the Europeans at pursuing an independent monetary policy, this was to become a source of conflict with the Americans.

The United Kingdom, on the other hand, suffered a deep recession beginning in 1980, as a consequence of fiscal and monetary restraint administered by the new Conservative government. Prime Minister Thatcher's fiscal course brought the budget into surplus on a cyclically adjusted basis within a few years.[37] A confirmed monetarist, Margaret Thatcher successfully resisted demands for reflation coming from almost the entire political spectrum, except the right wing of her party, as the recession wore on. In Germany, the twin deficit problem put the coalition government of the Social Democratic Party (SPD) and the Free Democratic Party (FDP) on the defensive. It responded by reducing the federal budget deficit, a process that was irreconcilably to divide the coalition. Until the budget and current account deficits could be reduced, the Bundesbank felt constrained to use monetary policy to defend the mark on the foreign currency markets, despite arguments by many that it should be directed against unemployment.

French President François Mitterrand instituted a distinctly Keynesian macroeconomic program in 1981 designed to redistribute income and sustain short-term growth through increases in welfare and other current expenditures, offset, in part, by tax increases on upper incomes. Employment was the primary socialist objective; Mitterrand was publicly complacent about inflation remaining at double-figure levels.[38] The Bank of

France, under the firm control of the Finance Ministry, initially pursued an easy money policy under the new government. Recognizing that these policies were out of step with those of the United States and its European partners, the government imposed strict foreign exchange and capital controls in an unsuccessful effort to avert a run on the franc.

With the important exception of France, fiscal balances tended to move in the opposite direction in the United States and elsewhere in the OECD world. Further, with the exception of the United Kingdom, the Europeans and Japanese had a strong preference for more expansionary monetary policy than that which the United States was pursuing. These opposite *mixes* were the primary source of conflict among governments during the 1981–83 period. The Europeans might have maintained a more independent monetary policy had they not been concerned about the adverse effects of currency depreciation. But, particularly since inflation was still fairly high in 1981–82, they were unwilling to let their currencies depreciate quickly and fluctuate greatly against the dollar. Without parroting every rate change, they moved their own interest rates more or less with American rates. Ironically, the Europeans thought that one means of achieving a decoupling in the markets between American interest rates and their own was to reduce further their fiscal deficits, thus aggravating the transatlantic differences over fiscal policy.

American 'Domesticism' and Non-intervention[39]

Concerted central bank intervention in the foreign exchange markets was believed by many Europeans to be another possible way of decoupling European from American monetary policy. Were currency depreciation not imminent, central banks would have greater scope to adopt independent monetary policies. The effectiveness of European intervention depended, however, in large measure on U.S. participation and the Reagan administration made clear that it viewed foreign exchange intervention as an attempt to circumvent the 'magic of the marketplace.' Officials at the Federal Reserve believed that intervention could, in fact, be effective under particular market conditions. The State Department advised that, in any case, non-intervention should not be a declared public policy because

15

the threat of intervention could be useful in reducing volatility in the market. Nevertheless, in April 1981, Treasury Secretary Donald Regan announced that the United States would not intervene in the foreign exchange markets except in extraordinary circumstances, such as the shooting of the President.[40] In testimony before Congress, his Undersecretary for Monetary Affairs, Beryl Sprinkel, explained that the administration regarded foreign exchange intervention as treatment of the symptom of more fundamental problems which could be fully and permanently corrected only by changing basic policies.[41]

The Europeans, who were not consulted in the course of the Treasury decision, were offended and angry. Their position was that, while it might be true that the fundamental stance of fiscal and monetary policy would determine exchange rates over the long run, intervention could reduce short-term volatility and possibly influence market expectations for longer periods as well. Even if intervention were not effective, governments should not announce publicly that speculators need not fear the stabilizing entry of the central banks into the markets. While there were important differences among the British, Germans, and French regarding the potential effectiveness of intervention, all felt that the Reagan administration had made a serious and callous error.

The U.S. Treasury agreed that unsterilized intervention would indeed change the exchange rate, but argued that this was the same as changing underlying monetary policy. The administration recognized, rightly, that monetary policy was the crux of the intervention issue. To the extent that the United States would intervene in a way that could really affect the international value of the dollar, it would be changing American monetary policy and, more importantly, 'bailing out,' in its view, foreign governments from their inflationary mistakes.

Foreign criticism of American policies was directed also at the high level of nominal interest rates, which remained between 15 and 16 percent during the summer of 1981, as measured by the U.S. prime rate. Chancellor Helmut Schmidt is said to have complained to a meeting of finance and economic ministers that real interest rates were the highest in Germany 'since the birth of Christ.' German Economics Minister Otto Graf Lambsdorff declared that Reagan had chosen the wrong means in his laudable fight against inflation. Lambsdorff said that the United States should rely less on monetary policy and more on tighter

16

fiscal policy, in other words, that it should change the policy mix.[42]

Initially, the Europeans and the Japanese did not speak with a single voice. The British in particular were less critical of the Americans; Thatcher's monetarist policies and spending reduction objectives resembling those of the Reagan administration. As a consequence, no important differences were resolved at the economic summit meeting in Ottawa in July 1981. Although the Europeans and Japanese expressed their concern about the emerging U.S. policy mix, Reagan could argue, with some sympathy from the others, that his policies should be given a chance to work. Over the course of the following year, however, the Europeans and Japanese became increasingly unified in their objections to U.S. policy. At the 1982 summit at Versailles, Reagan was virtually isolated on the questions of the American policy mix and the dollar.

Newly cognizant of foreign consternation, Reagan sounded the keynote of his administration's international economic policy in an address to the World Bank and International Monetary Fund (IMF) 1981 annual meeting, saying: 'The most important contribution any country can make to world development is to pursue sound economic policies at home.'[43] Acknowledging that the President and his economic advisers had concentrated primarily on the domestic objectives of his program, Undersecretary Sprinkel argued that the program would restore confidence in the dollar, contribute to stability in international financial markets and foreign growth, and dissipate protectionist pressures.[44]

Multilateral Surveillance

Transatlantic economic diplomacy in the winter of 1981–82 dropped to its lowest point since the Nixon administration had unilaterally suspended gold convertibility and imposed the import surcharge more than a decade earlier. In this antagonistic atmosphere, the G-7 countries began to prepare for the Versailles summit meeting. The Americans were acutely conscious that the French had made the U.S. refusal to intervene in exchange markets a symbol of American unwillingness to cooperate. American strategy was to transcend these arguments by focusing instead on the 'fundamentals' in the summit

17

countries. (It was never clear exactly what 'fundamentals' referred to: policy or performance. It appeared, by the use of the term, that intervention, trade protectionism and, most importantly, the current account balance and the exchange rate were not 'fundamentals.') By so doing, Reagan administration officials aimed to accomplish two things. First, they hoped to induce change in other governments' policies, particularly the French. Second, they wished to deflect criticism from American policy over the rise of the dollar. They, therefore, proposed to their counterparts that the Article IV bilateral consultations between the IMF and member governments be 'multilateralized' among summit countries.

Exchange rates were determined by fundamentals, Treasury officials reasoned, and would fluctuate only if fundamentals diverged among countries. The Treasury, thus, promulgated a doctrine of 'convergence.'[45] Secretary Regan stated that the American goal at the Versailles summit would be 'a convergence of our economies with each more stable and with less inflation. If that happens,' he added 'that will stabilize exchange rates.'[46] Undersecretary Sprinkel was more direct:

If [the Europeans] want to opt for slower inflation and more real growth as we're doing, we certainly would welcome it. But if they don't opt in that direction, it's understandable their exchange rates are going to decline vis-à-vis the dollar.[47]

While disagreeing with American non-intervention policy, the Germans were sympathetic to the view that monetary and fiscal policy, growth and inflation were fundamental determinants of exchange rates and current account positions. When in 1982, Mitterrand proposed a 'decoupling' of European from American interest rates, the Germans rejected the idea, suspicious that they would have to finance expansionary French policies under the plan. Nor were the British interested in the scheme: it would have entailed joining the European Monetary System (EMS), formally or informally, which Thatcher steadfastly opposed, as well as extensive capital controls. Neither government was willing to enter into such an arrangement with the French and believed that Mitterrand would have to change his underlying policies to stem downward pressure on the franc; multilateral surveillance might be a mechanism to convince him to do so. More importantly, however, the Europeans regarded multilateral surveillance as a potentially useful lever to convince the Reagan administration to act on the budget deficit.

The Americans could not get agreement on multilateral surveillance at the summit, however, without yielding somewhat on their strong anti-intervention position. A compromise was negotiated by Sprinkel and his French counterpart, Michel Camdessus, at one of the preparatory meetings of the personal representatives of the summiteers. Their agreement, acceded to by the other 'sherpas,' hinged on two points. The Americans agreed to reaffirm their commitment to intervene in disorderly exchange markets, and to conduct a study with the other summit countries on the effectiveness of exchange intervention. The other governments agreed to convene the G-5 finance ministers with the Managing Director of the IMF to work for 'greater stability of the world monetary system.' They omitted any guide as to how policy adjustment might be assigned, however. The monetary annex to the final Versailles communiqué simply stated: 'We recognise that [greater stability of the world monetary system] rests primarily on convergence of policies designed to achieve lower inflation, higher employment and renewed economic growth ... .' Furthermore, violent disagreement after the summit revealed that in agreeing to conduct the study the U.S. Treasury had not in fact changed American intervention policy.[48] Despite the controversy, the agreement to study intervention and conduct multilateral surveillance in the G-5 survived.

As an institution already in existence, the G-5 was ready-made to house the new consultations. The G-5 had previously included central bank governors in their meetings and this practice continued as the Group took on new responsibilities. From this Group, however, three summit participants were excluded: the Canadians, the Italians, and officials of the European Community (EC). These groups acceded to the agreement without strong protest, perhaps perceiving the important part of the monetary accord to be the intervention study, not multilateral surveillance. They were not eager, moreover, to subject their policies to broader surveillance. In 1985, however, they were to object firmly to their exclusion.

The new process started without the Italians and Canadians with the first conference in Toronto, in September 1982. The meetings revolved around the presentation of a paper by the Managing Director of the IMF, Jacques de Larosière, examining

19

economic conditions and policy settings in each country. The presentations were reportedly hard-hitting, confronting the finance ministers and central bankers with their major policy problems. The Group was supposedly most critical of the American and French budget deficits during its sessions in Toronto and the following spring in Washington, before the Williamsburg summit.[49] None of these papers or discussions was made public, however, in keeping with the secretiveness of the G-5. This meant that the value of the Group was limited to the direct effects it had on its members: a fuller appreciation of the international impact of their policies, and better understanding of the problems and policies of others. The Group's greatest contribution over the year following Versailles was its coordination of international financial policy with respect to debtor countries and the IMF, rather than multilateral surveillance.

The Versailles intervention study was concluded in advance of the Williamsburg summit, as planned. In the course of the study, the French genuinely moderated their views on the effectiveness of intervention. The study concluded that sterilized intervention would not be effective in altering exchange rates in the longer term, but that coordinated intervention could be useful in reducing short-run volatility.[50] Incorporated into the Williamsburg communiqué, it stated:

> We agree to pursue closer consultations on policies affecting exchange markets and on market conditions. While retaining our freedom to operate independently, we are willing to undertake coordinated intervention in exchange markets in instances where it is agreed that such intervention would be helpful.

At Williamsburg, the heads of government assigned their finance ministers to a second study, spawned by Mitterrand's call for a 'new Bretton Woods,' on 'defining the conditions for improving the international monetary system and to consider the part which might, in due course, be played in this process by a high-level international monetary conference.' The summit also reinforced the G-5 commitment to multilateral surveillance and specified the policies and objectives with which these consultations would be concerned.[51]

The Costs of Conflict

Failing to agree on policy adjustments, the governments could only agree on form and procedure. Those procedures were potentially quite important; the institutional framework laid at Versailles and Williamsburg was later used seriously. At the beginning of 1984, however, very little, if any, mutual adjustment of macroeconomic policies had taken place among the G-5 countries during the first Reagan administration. Fiscal policy in the United States continued to diverge dramatically from fiscal policy in Europe and Japan.[52] At Williamsburg there was agreement that emphasis should be given to reduce spending in order to lower deficits. But that did not mute unanimous criticism by the other governments of U.S. budget deficits, the projections for which were rising. President Reagan's reply was that he too was opposed to U.S. deficits; but it was clear that reducing them was not his top priority.

Monetary policies among the summit countries tended to move broadly in parallel. But, with others following the American lead, this could hardly be described as *mutual* adjustment. American monetary loosening in mid-1982 permitted a general easing of monetary conditions worldwide and, in combination with the fiscal stimulus, generated the U.S. recovery. But American real interest rates remained high, giving grounds for continued criticism of U.S. interest rate policy by the Europeans. The dollar, furthermore, continued a relentless upward climb.

With adjustment deferred, the largest share of the political costs of conflict was borne by the Europeans. International macroeconomic conflict contributed to domestic political conflict in Germany and undermined the French Socialist government. In Britain, in early 1983, real Gross Domestic Product (GDP) remained 5 percent below the level at which it had been when the Conservatives took power, and unemployment figures remained around 3 million, well into double percentage figures. Prime Minister Thatcher, however, was spared the political consequences of adverse macroeconomic performance by two favorable political developments. First, the Falkland Islands War gave Thatcher an opportunity to exercise decisive leadership, and Britain's swift victory boosted her popularity. Second, the Labour Party was deeply divided by the search for a credible alternative to her policies. The schism immobilized the party and provoked a number of members on the right to join the newly formed Social Democratic Party (SDP), which allied itself with the Liberal Party. The SDP-Liberal alliance changed the British political landscape radically. During the parliamentary elections in June 1983, the new alliance split the vote with Labour to allow the Conservatives an overwhelming majority in the House of Commons, despite virtually no improvement in the Conservatives' percentage of the popular vote over 1979.

In Germany, the SPD-FDP government was less fortunate. Unemployment rose to 2.5 million (roughly 9 percent of the labor force) in January 1983, the highest absolute level since 1950. These levels, among other issues, radicalized the left wing of the SPD, prompting the FDP to break from the coalition in autumn 1982 and join the conservative coalition of the Christian Democratic Union and the Christian Social Union (CDU-CSU) to form a new government. The new coalition, under the leadership of Helmut Kohl, received a governing majority in the Bundestag elections of March 1983. Kohl and his Finance Minister, Gerhard Stoltenberg, proceeded to tighten fiscal policy further. Maintaining relatively restrictive monetary policies made this task more difficult and worsened the coalition's relations with the trade unions.

The French Socialists sustained a precipitous decline in popularity as a result of disappointing macroeconomic performance and the consequent switch to austerity policies. As much of the stimulus to domestic demand in 1982 leaked abroad through deterioration in the trade balance, unemployment continued to rise while inflation remained almost 10 percent. In early 1983, Mitterrand faced perhaps the most important decision of his term: whether to close the borders of the French economy by further tightening capital and exchange controls, withdrawing from the EMS, and protecting sectors exposed to international competition, or to repudiate, in effect, the economic program of his first two years. He chose to keep France within the liberal international economic system, at great political cost. The retrenchment from expansionary policies necessitated a cabinet reorganization, provoked a general crisis of confidence within the country and set the stage for the withdrawal of the Communist Party from the coalition. Mitterrand's popular approval rating dropped from 74 percent in June 1982 to 35 percent in July 1983.[53] The Socialists never fully recovered from this setback.

In contrast, the Reagan administration, not having changed the basic course of policy, retained important coalition members and remained popular. In 1983, the full impact of administration tax and spending policies on the budget deficit became apparent, with the red ink totaling $195 billion in that year. Washington remained deeply divided over the solution to, and indeed the seriousness of, these deficits. Herbert Stein aptly described American fiscal policy under the first Reagan administration:

Although everyone said that the big deficits were bad, hardly anyone was willing to give up anything he valued very much in order to reduce them. That was as true of President Reagan as of anyone else. His attitude was decisive. If the most 'conservative' President in fifty years would not make any sacrifice in order to avoid the biggest deficits in history, who would?[54]

Criticism of the United States came from a wide number of governments abroad, ranging from the French Socialist government to the otherwise sympathetic British Conservative government and the generally inoffensive Japanese. All were critical of the U.S. federal budget deficit, viewing Reagan's endorsement of a balanced budget amendment to the U.S. constitution as sanctimonious. Mitterrand had suffered greatest politically among foreign leaders from macroeconomic conflict but he echoed the sentiment of other leaders when in autumn 1983 he said, 'I overestimated the goodwill of the Americans. I don't expect anything any more from Reagan.'[55]

IV
The Reflation
Controversy of 1984-86

During 1984, the American recovery strengthened while U.S. inflation remained moderate. Growth rebounded in Japan as well but the European economies remained sluggish and unemployment continued to climb. Europe's less favorable growth performance drained the force from European complaints about high American real interest rates. Europe, in fact, benefited from a large increase in net exports to the United States. Furthermore, 1984 was an election year for Reagan, and foreign governments were very reluctant to intervene in the American domestic debate on budgets and taxes against the popular incumbent. At the London economic summit in June of that year, Prime Minister Thatcher lavished praise on the American President for the successful U.S. recovery.

The American Offensive

With the help of economic recovery, public criticism of American policies by foreign governments seemed to be effectively stifled. Even the French began to promote free market policies, adopting positions on flexibility in labor markets and the role of price incentives, indistinguishable from those of more conservative governments.[56] The Europeans and Japanese continued to argue that continuing large U.S. budget deficits risked economic stagnation, inflation, or both in the long term, but the Reagan administration had won a remarkable ideological victory in achieving virtually unanimous agreement on free market principles among the seven summit countries.

Convergence of growth and inflation performance, however,

remained elusive. National inflation rates ranged from 3.9 percent for Japan to 11.1 for France and 16.1 for Italy in 1984.[57] While the U.S. economy grew 6.6 percent, and the Japanese economy grew 5.1 percent, that of the European OECD countries, as a group, grew only 2.6 percent. Unemployment continued to rise in Europe, averaging 10.8 percent, and was projected to rise gradually at a time when it was dropping in the United States and Japan. These divergent trends in the labor markets reversed the long standing pattern throughout the 1960s and 1970s where European unemployment was characteristically lower than American joblessness. Since 1974, the U.S. economy had created roughly 15 million new jobs, while Europe had actually lost 2 million jobs on a net basis.[58] The comparison indicated that there were long-term investment and labor market problems in Europe, a syndrome dubbed 'Eurosclerosis.'

Propelled by the influx of capital, the dollar continued to appreciate against the yen and European currencies in 1984. The expensive dollar, and differentials in the growth of domestic demand among the United States, Japan, and Europe, produced increases in the American current account deficit, which had already risen from a slight deficit in 1982 to $41 billion in 1983, and registered $107 billion in 1984. The growing external deficit acted, sometimes strongly, as a drag on U.S. GNP, reducing the real annual growth rate in the third quarter of 1984 by nearly 4 points to 1.9 percent.[59]

Emboldened by the resounding victory for the President in the November elections, the administration began to act more aggressively in macroeconomic policy conflict. Concerned that the European stagnation could be damaging not only to Europe's economies in the long term, but also to world recovery and, ultimately, to alliance security, the administration initiated a broad assault on the welfare state.[60] The scope of this offensive went far beyond recommendations on macroeconomic policy, such as tax cuts, to prescriptions for increasing labor market flexibility, reducing the role of government through state-owned enterprises, eliminating subsidies to private firms, and generally unleashing price and profit incentives. These prescriptions struck at the core interests of major social and economic groups forming the postwar political consensus in several European states.[61] This assault proved to be short lived, however, as the more conservative items on this agenda faded

25

into the background. What remained at the center of the second Reagan administration's foreign economic strategy was the effort to persuade the Europeans and Japanese to undertake expansionary changes in foreign monetary and fiscal policies to stimulate domestic demand in their countries. Supply-side principles receded and monetarism dropped away, leaving administration policies with a distinctly Keynesian emphasis on demand management, and bearing a strong resemblance to the strategy of the Carter administration during the 'locomotive' conflict of 1977–78.

Yen-Dollar Agreement

In the first half of 1984, the administration's attention focused mainly on Japan and the issue of capital market liberalization. The Treasury's position coincided with its general free market principles. It also coincided with the interests of American financial institutions which wanted to tap the Japanese markets as a source of funds and were better prepared to take full advantage of new market opportunities at the time than potential Japanese competitors. More importantly, U.S. pressure on the Japanese government to eliminate capital controls coincided with increasing concern on the part of the Treasury and the Fed about the feasibility of financing burgeoning American current account deficits.

The financial liberalization issue arose from a bilateral dispute over the yen-dollar exchange rate — which stood at 232 yen per dollar at the beginning of 1984 — during which the Japanese uncharacteristically criticized the large U.S. budget deficit as responsible for the high value of the dollar. Americans argued that the dollar was not high but the yen was too low, allegedly the result of domestic credit regulations that kept Japanese interest rates low.[62] They prescribed a liberalization of Japanese capital markets to correct the problem. A yen-dollar committee was convened in February 1984 to examine this question. Benefiting from a split within the Japanese financial community on the issue, Secretary Regan reached an agreement with Finance Minister Noboru Takeshita a couple of weeks prior to the London summit.[63] The agreement was unbalanced. The Japanese were obligated to take the most important measures. While Regan pledged to try to reduce the federal

26

budget deficit, his obligations were not spelled out with the specificity of the Japanese commitments.[64]

The American bilateral trade deficit with Japan continued to widen throughout 1984 reaching $37 billion for the year. In early 1985, President Reagan and Prime Minister Yasuhiro Nakasone discussed this issue, as well as related trade and other foreign policy questions. They agreed to work toward better balance in U.S.-Japanese trade and economic relations. Nakasone added: 'To this end Japan will promote economic policies that will enhance growth led by domestic private demand and will make further market opening efforts.'[65] His emphasis on private demand indicated that fiscal policy would not be expanded to ameliorate conflict.

Dollar Bubble

At the end of 1984, the British pound came under intensified downward pressure, prompted in part by sagging oil prices. It had been dropping steadily against the dollar since the second quarter, reaching a new low of $1.16 at the end of the year. In mid-January 1985, Thatcher reportedly wrote to Reagan stressing their friendship and asking for his help in curbing the decline of her currency.[66] Having countenanced a recent 4.5 percent increase in interest rates at home, she reiterated this request during a visit to Washington in mid-February, as the pound neared parity with the dollar.[67] That such a strong opponent to tying the pound to the EMS, and supporter of the U.S. position on international monetary questions, should ask for American help on the exchange rate is significant. The American response, interpreted by the British press as a slap in the face, was equally telling. During Thatcher's visit, Reagan stated that other countries should undertake more to increase their growth rather than demand that the United States attempt to bring down the value of the dollar.[68]

A few days later, the continued rapid appreciation of the dollar against all currencies provoked the verbal intervention of the Fed Chairman, Paul Volcker. On 25 February, the dollar reached the highest levels for decades against most currencies: 262.55 yen, 3.44 marks, and $1.05 to the pound. In congressional testimony the next day, Volcker announced that central bank intervention had not been forceful enough against the dollar, and that he did not like either the volatility or direction of the change.[69] This marked an important modification in Volcker's public pronouncements on intervention. Always concerned about the high value of the dollar, the current account deficit and potential problems of financing it, he had previously stressed the primacy of more fundamental market forces.[70]

From the beginning to 26 February, the dollar had appreciated nearly 10 percent against the major European currencies, and 3 percent against the yen. The Fed intervened three times, selling a total of $208.6 million for marks, $97.6 million for yen, and $16.8 million for sterling. After the peak, the Fed sold $257.2 million for marks in late February and early March. Volcker's statements and concerted intervention brought the dollar down from its high levels, and it continued to depreciate without U.S. intervention through mid-April, by 15 percent against the mark and 4 percent against the yen. During February and early March, the Fed sold roughly $500 million for marks, yen and sterling.[71] Coordinated with the other G-5 central banks, total intervention was the largest for a number of years.

Meanwhile, the report on the international monetary system, requested at the Williamsburg summit, had to take stock of this volatility in the markets. The report, which was given to the deputies of the G-10 finance ministers to carry out, was due for completion prior to the Bonn summit.[72] But, in fact, the work carried over into the month of June. Led by the French, some of the deputies favored proposals to introduce target zones or 'references rates.' However, the report concluded: 'the adoption of target zones is undesirable and in any case impractical in current circumstances.' The deputies considered ways of strengthening multilateral surveillance, agreeing that it had not been 'as effective as desirable in influencing national policies and in promoting underlying economic and financial conditions conducive to exchange rate stability.' But it concluded that no major changes were required in the institutional arrangements for surveillance; only that governments should use those mechanisms to greater effect.[73]

The Money-Trade Link

The question of international monetary reform figured prominently at the summit held in Bonn in May 1985. In order to coax the French to accede to EC approval of a date for commencement of a new round of GATT negotiations, Secretary James Baker proposed a high-level meeting to consider the international monetary system.[74] The agenda for this meeting was limited to the conclusions of the G-10 report and did not include major monetary reform. Other EC members believed they had French agreement on the *quid pro quo*, but mindful that French agricultural interests in the EC were at stake should agriculture be placed on the GATT agenda, and of upcoming elections for the National Assembly in 1986, Mitterrand rejected the package deal at the summit.

The linkage between the trade and monetary areas had been made in the United States as well. In advance of the summit, Senators Danforth and Bentsen explicitly linked their approval of a new GATT round to inclusion of monetary issues. Danforth was emphatic:

> Congress should insist on clear plans for rectifying the exchange-rate problem ... as conditions for granting the president ... authority for implementing a new negotiating round .... No trade policy can work if the exchange rate problem is not resolved.[75]

Their proposals were harbingers of growing congressional insistence that the value of the dollar be a deliberate target of administration policy, rather than a residual afterthought.

The outcry in Congress on the trade issue rose to a crescendo during the summer, provoked by a combination of an increasing trade deficit and almost cavalier administration inattention to the issue. Hundreds of trade bills were presented by members, some of which gathered formidable support in both houses. A typical example of these bills was one which aimed to reduce significantly the discretionary power of the Fed and the Treasury in international monetary policy, requiring the United States to intervene in the foreign exchange markets when the current account balance was in substantial deficit.[76]

Confrontation

Despite depreciation from the level reached in February, the dollar remained vastly overvalued in the summer of 1985. Estimates of the overvaluation of the real effective exchange rate for the dollar ranged between 22 and 49 percent, and much higher against some individual currencies.[77] At these exchange rates, the major econometric models showed that the American current account deficit would grow and remain substantial for years, on the assumption that foreign fiscal and monetary policies remained unchanged.[78] Amid these projections, there was great concern in the United States and abroad that, as U.S. external debt mounted, foreign investors would at some point refuse to lend further to the United States, precipitating a flight from dollar-denominated assets, an uncontrolled dollar depreciation, a tightening of American monetary policy, and a world recession.[79] Conscious of this scenario, the Bank for International Settlements (BIS) observed in its annual report that the problem before the advanced capitalist states was how to 'secure a smooth unwinding of the U.S external imbalance.'[80]

There was no agreement, however, among the G-5 governments on what action should be taken; in particular, whether it would be sufficient for the United States to reduce its budget deficit or if it was also necessary for Japan and the surplus countries of Europe to stimulate growth through tax cuts or market liberalization measures of their own. While there were important divisions within all countries on fiscal policy, each government ultimately adopted the position that would require the *others* to take fiscal action. This was as true of the Reagan administration as other governments. President Reagan himself acknowledged in February that: 'the trade deficit is like the budget deficit; both are too large to be sustained,' but did not change his basic fiscal strategy.[81] Even Volcker, a persistent advocate of reducing the United States' budget deficit, advised foreign countries to stimulate their domestic economies by 'speeding tax reductions' and other measures.[82]

Plaza Accord and Dollar Depreciation

The protectionist outcry on Capitol Hill and flagging American growth, however, impressed upon the Reagan administration

30

the need for decisive action. Under the leadership of Secretary Baker, the administration embarked on a new period in its foreign economic policy which consciously sought the 'smooth unwinding' of the U.S. current account deficit with continued world growth. Previously, Treasury officials operated on the belief that strong foreign growth was necessary for appreciation of foreign currencies. But in 1985, they became convinced that a depreciation of the dollar was desirable and feasible even if the Japanese and European governments did not stimulate demand. The two-year effort then launched by Baker was characterized by an uneasy mix of cooperation and discord among the major countries. While its ultimate accomplishments are still unclear, the administration sought successfully to depress the value of the dollar, reduce world interest rates, and avoid a reversal of capital inflows into the United States before the current deficit could be reduced.

Baker's first major step was to develop an international accord declaring unanimous support for continuing but orderly depreciation of the dollar. That agreement was announced at the September meeting of the G-5 at the Plaza Hotel in New York. The negotiations leading up to this event were shrouded in secrecy, to give the final declaration the maximum possible impact, and to conceal areas of fundamental disagreement. It has been reported that during these discussions, initiated bilaterally several months before the Plaza meeting, Baker tried to get agreement on foreign stimulus but failed. He got agreement, nonetheless, on dollar depreciation and presented the communiqué with a fanfare uncharacteristic of the G-5 at an unprecedented press conference.[83]

The finance ministers and central bank governors of the Five observed that their national growth rates were expected to be more balanced than at any time in the last four years. But, their communiqué read, these conditions 'have not been reflected fully in exchange markets.' They concluded that 'some further orderly appreciation of the main non-dollar currencies against the dollar is desirable,' and indicated that '[they] stand ready to cooperate more closely to encourage this when to do so would be helpful.' Each minister then attached a list of policy measures which his government would pursue to 'improve the fundamentals further.'[84]

The markets responded dramatically, as the dollar registered its largest one-day drop against the yen and mark since the transition to floating exchange rates. On an effective basis, it fell 4.3 percent the Monday after the Plaza announcement.[85] Yet, although Baker achieved agreement that the dollar should depreciate, there was little agreement on exactly how far it should fall. Within little more than two weeks, having seen the dollar drop 7 percent against the mark (down to 2.65 marks to the dollar), Bundesbank President, Karl Otto Poehl, announced that the dollar had reached a level 'that is acceptable to us,' intending to arrest the slide.[86] Baker's Assistant Secretary for International Affairs later complained that Germany had been the 'least responsive' of the Five to the Plaza accord, and that Germany had 'not satisfied' the administration.[87] Poehl responded by saying that too much had been interpreted into the agreement, and that the G-5 had entered into no commitments or agreements of any sort to move toward a system of target zones.

More fundamentally, however, no government agreed to change monetary or fiscal policy under the Plaza agreement. Most finance ministers returned home and declared that the agreement did not imply any change of policy for them. Moreover, they continued to call for adjustment on the part of the others.[88] The Japanese government, however, proved to be considerably more cooperative than the German government during the following months. In late October, the Japanese tightened monetary policy significantly in order to ensure the continued appreciation of the yen. Prime Minister Nakasone, in contrast to the Germans, reaffirmed 'efforts to see the yen appreciate' even after an 11 percent appreciation against the dollar.[89]

Domestic Developments

Important developments were taking place, meanwhile, within the leading countries. In the United States, agreement had been reached, in August, on a significant package of government spending reductions. In December, the Congress passed and the President signed the Gramm-Rudman-Hollings Bill which aimed to reduce progressively the federal budget deficit to zero by the end of the decade. Although the constitutionality of the new legislation was in doubt, there was hope that a sea change in the politics of fiscal policy was taking place in

Washington. While the administration managed to stave off protectionism in Congress in autumn 1985, the Democrats promised to make it an election issue by passing a trade bill through the House in the spring.

In Japan, the government announced over the summer an 'action program' to raise domestic demand, and implemented a supplementary budget in October. With these measures in place, government officials were divided as to whether they should do more. The Ministry of International Trade and Industry (MITI), the Economic Planning Agency (EPA), and even the Bank of Japan seemed to be leaning in the direction of a greater fiscal stimulus, as were some factions of the Liberal Democratic Party (LDP). Finance Minister Takeshita, on the other hand, stood resolutely opposed to increases in government spending or significant tax reductions.

Within Germany, tax cuts amounting to DM 10 billion were planned for 1986, with another round of roughly equal magnitude for 1988. As these tax cuts merely compensated for fiscal drag occurring over the preceding years, support developed within Germany to implement the 1988 cuts ahead of schedule, as many foreigners were advising. The SPD opposition and some members of the governing coalition advocated that both stages be implemented in 1986.[90] The five federally supported economic research institutes called for implementation of the 1988 cuts in 1987.[91] Finance Minister Stoltenberg firmly rejected these arguments, a position shared by Poehl.[92]

Despite domestic political developments which seemed to offer hope for international cooperation, fiscal and monetary policies were not adjusting so as to ameliorate payments imbalances in the near future. Moreover, even Japanese acquiescence in yen appreciation began to evaporate. In early 1986, the dollar continued to fall against both the mark and the yen. The Bank of Japan reversed its earlier tightening of monetary policy and Takeshita indicated that he too was comfortable with the yen at current levels — then at 180 yen to the dollar. While they initially agreed with the Baker initiative, neither Germany nor Japan wanted their currencies to appreciate enough to reduce net exports rapidly, as this would cause domestic political problems arising from reduced growth and increased unemployment.

A visible and significant change in trade balances, however, was exactly what both Baker and Volcker needed in order to dampen trade protectionism. Consequently, neither would publicly sanction exchange rates that would not bring substantial adjustment of the current account, and those levels were not approached in early 1986. On the other hand, they had to avoid creating the expectation of a rapid, continuous depreciation of the dollar in order to avoid flight from dollar-denominated assets. The two U.S. officials, thus, walked a tightrope after the Plaza accord. Volcker occasionally expressed his concern that the dollar should not fall too quickly, but refused to state what his preferred levels were. Baker refused to concede that the depreciation had been sufficient, but stressed that he did not want to see a 'free fall' of the dollar. While at times their public comments seemed to be at odds, their combined statements served to orchestrate a record depreciation of the dollar without causing panic in the markets.

Joint Interest Rate Reductions

Withholding exchange rate stabilization was particularly important in the light of mediocre growth prospects for the United States in early 1986. In order to sustain capital inflows while reducing the American discount rate, the United States needed to persuade other governments to lower their interest rates as well. Baker urged joint discount rate reductions on the other G-5 members during the preparations for their January meeting in London, threatening further depreciation of the dollar as one means of persuasion. Thus began an alternating process of dollar depreciation followed by interest rate reductions, in one-half percent decrements.

The result was a worldwide easing of monetary conditions. The Bank of Japan, alone, lowered its discount rate from 5.0 to 4.5 percent at the end of January 1986, to stem appreciation of the yen. Amid much discord, the Fed, Bundesbank, and Bank of Japan together lowered discount rates one-half point in March. The Fed, with the Bank of Japan, then lowered discount rates in April, and again, alone, in July and August. As part of a temporary exchange rate stabilization accord arranged between Baker and the new Japanese finance minister, Kiichi Miyazawa, the Bank of Japan again lowered the discount rate at the end of October, and then again in February 1987. The German Bundesbank offered greater resistance, but conceded a discount rate cut again in January 1987, after a realignment of the EMS failed to stabilize the system. Between January 1986 and February 1987, discount rates were lowered from 7.5 to 5.5 percent in the United States, from 5.0 to 2.5 percent in Japan, and 4.0 to 3.0 percent in Germany.

Baker used the prospect of further depreciation of the dollar to urge the Germans and Japanese onward during this process. When in the summer of 1986, for example, the Bundesbank and Bank of Japan demurred, he declared that the dollar would have to fall further unless the Germans and Japanese took measures to raise domestic demand.[93] The linkage between the dollar and foreign demand was echoed by virtually every important American economic official, including Volcker.[94] These statements put considerable downward pressure on the dollar in the foreign exchange markets. By making clear to the markets his willingness to see the dollar depreciate, Baker confronted his foreign counterparts with a choice between reducing interest rates or countenancing future declines in net exports. But, from the American point of view, while the general loosening of monetary policy would tend to sustain growth in the G-5, only a greater increase in domestic demand outside the United States, or a further currency correction, could reduce the current account imbalances. Without assurances of further demand stimulation in Germany and Japan, Baker would not surrender his option to nudge the dollar lower still.

Tokyo Summit 1986: Enhanced Multilateral Surveillance

Secretary Baker and his deputy, Richard Darman, used the economic summit meeting in Tokyo, in May 1986, to advance a proposal for a framework for better coordination of macro-economic policies. Approaching their counterparts from each of the major countries in turn, they reached agreement not on a specific coordination package but on a remarkable *process* of macroeconomic policy coordination, fortifying the multilateral surveillance machinery already in place. The agreement, announced by the heads of government in Tokyo, strengthened multilateral surveillance in four ways.[95]

First, national economic forecasts were to be reviewed collectively with a view to examining their mutual compatibility

35

by reference to a specific list of indicators. Second, when 'significant deviations' developed from the 'intended course' of the G-5 economies, the Five were to 'make their best efforts to reach an understanding on appropriate remedial measures' in the multilateral surveillance exercise. Third, a new Group of Seven finance ministers was created in order to include the Canadians and Italians in the review of economic objectives and forecasts and when 'the improvement of the international monetary system and related economic policy measures' would be discussed. Finally, the central role of the IMF and its Managing Director in multilateral surveillance was reaffirmed. Compelled to come to grips with the problem of assigning the responsibility for adjustment to individual governments, the summit countries resurrected an indicators system reminiscent of the 'objective indicators' proposal to the Committee of Twenty in the early 1970s.

It was clear, however, that the agreement on the new process was a second-best substitute for agreement on policy coordination. The commitment of the summit countries to enhanced surveillance was in doubt, and the practical details on how it might actually work were murky. Meeting several times over the summer, the G-5 deputies addressed these details to put arrangements in place prior to the next gathering of their ministers at the annual meeting of the World Bank and IMF in Washington at the end of September. As operationalized, the new process was circumscribed by the incomparability of data submitted by each finance ministry, the narrowness of the circle of national officials involved in the exercise, and the limited role that the IMF staff was permitted to play in offering independent recommendations. To date, the process has not provided a standard against which the need for remedial measures can be judged. Nonetheless, enhanced multilateral surveillance remains in place and could yet serve the G-5 or G-7 governments as the basis for a macroeconomic regime.

Japan Responds to U.S. Pressure

In anticipation of hosting the 1986 G-7 summit, Nakasone commissioned a group of experts to produce a report on Japanese foreign economic relations. That group, chaired by former Bank of Japan Governor, Haruo Maekawa, presented its conclusions to the Prime Minister in April. It stated that Japan should stimulate domestic demand and indicated how it might take decisive action. While the report coincided closely with the American position, Reagan administration officials continued to press the Japanese strongly, asking pointed questions regarding specific measures to be taken. To satisfy the skeptics, Tokyo issued a statement detailing how 'structural adjustment' would be achieved, without quantifying the effects of the measures they specified.[96]

Meanwhile, Nakasone scored a resounding victory for the LDP in a 'double' election of the Diet and one-half of the House of Councillors in early July. Despite anxiety over the appreciation of the yen and fall in exports, the LDP won a record majority in the Diet, and Nakasone's own faction broadened as well. The LDP faction leaders thus consented to amending party rules to extend Nakasone's term by one year. In the ensuing cabinet reshuffle, Nakasone appointed the expansionist Keiichi Miyazawa Minister of Finance, and initiated a supplementary budget for passage through the Diet in September. The new government tried to satisfy the Americans without increasing the public deficit, and so announced measures to raise private domestic demand, principally through amendments in savings, housing, and land-use policies. The supplementary budget also accelerated public works expenditures. While the face value of the package was 1.3 percent of GNP, its actual effect was expected by private Japanese analysts and the U.S. Treasury to be considerably less.

The Americans welcomed the measures, nonetheless. With the Maekawa Report and then the new budget, the Japanese made every effort to appear as cooperative as possible — in stark contrast to the style of the Germans — and these changes held out hope for longer term increases in Japanese demand. Moreover, Japanese exports were suffering on a volume basis owing to the yen appreciation. The Reagan administration seemed temporarily satisfied with Japanese efforts.

Baker, therefore, agreed to call a temporary halt to the slide of the dollar against the yen at the end of October. He and Miyazawa agreed to state publicly that the exchange rate 'is now broadly consistent with the present underlying fundamentals.'[97] On the Japanese side, the Bank of Japan reduced its discount rate another step and submitted its supplementary budget to the Diet. Announced at the end of October, when the exchange rate was at 163 yen to the dollar, the agreement indicated that the United States would be content to see the rate roughly remain between 150 and 165. Frustrated at the lack of response on the part of the Germans, the United States concluded this separate bargain with the Japanese. Notably, the agreement invited the other members of the G-5 to join. But the price of a U.S. commitment to exchange rate stabilization was the demand for stimulative monetary and fiscal policies in the G-5 countries.

Germany Responds

As German demand surged in the second quarter of 1986, neither Bonn nor Frankfurt was keen on interest rate cuts or to bring forward the 1988 tax cuts to January 1987. The Bundesbank, which has always jealously guarded its independence from the federal government, not to mention foreign governments, was particularly concerned with the overshooting of the monetary growth targets. With national elections in January 1987 approaching, Stoltenberg did not want to expose himself to the charge that he had yielded to foreign pressure for a fiscal stimulus. The September meeting of the G-5 saw no accord between the Americans and Germans, except agreement that Baker would stop actively talking the dollar down and Bonn would reconsider its fiscal policy in early 1987 after the elections.

Although they opposed Baker's talking down the dollar, Germany's European partners favored stronger German demand. Furthermore, both the French and the Italians expressed interest in accepting Baker and Miyazawa's invitation to join their currency-stability accord. When the depreciation of the dollar and French labor disputes sparked a crisis within the EMS in January 1987, French Prime Minister, Jacques Chirac, bitterly complained that the Germans should do more to calm the markets.[98] The German government responded by revaluing the mark 3 percent within the EMS, along with the Dutch guilder. After the realignment proved insufficient to stem the crisis, the Bundesbank reduced the discount rate.

The German elections at the end of January were a dramatic success for the FDP, which had indicated during the campaign that an acceleration of the tax cuts was in order. As the CDU-CSU coalition lost vote share within the Bundestag, those in

38

favor of an early tax cut, as well as a more comprehensive, long-term tax reform, were strengthened in post-election intra-government bargaining. From outside the government, they continued to receive the support of the economic institutes, which anticipated lower rates of growth in 1987 owing to export short-falls, visible in the final quarter of 1986.[99] At a G-5 meeting in Paris four weeks after the election, Stoltenberg finally announced an increase in the size of the 1988 tax cut. A few days later, the coalition agreed on a more far-reaching tax reform plan scheduled for implementation in 1990.

The February G-5 meeting marked Stoltenberg's accession to the Baker-Miyazawa accord. The G-5 and Canada (controversy erupted over Italy's participation) listed monetary and fiscal measures that each country would undertake. Except for the Japanese discount rate reduction announced before the meeting, Germany's contribution was the only new undertaking in macroeconomic policy. But Stoltenberg refused to advance the date of the tax reduction into 1987, and tax reform in 1990 was far removed from the immediate problems of adjustment.

In exchange, the Americans agreed to 'cooperate closely to foster stability of exchange rates around current levels' (1.82 marks to the dollar), although no reference was made to joint intervention in their communiqué. In agreeing that exchange rates were 'broadly consistent with the underlying fundamentals,' Baker signaled that he would be ready to terminate the effort to depreciate the dollar initiated at the Plaza meeting. However, this clearly depended on Germany and Japan fulfilling their stated intentions to expand domestic demand. It remains to be seen whether the G-5 agreement will live up to the label 'Plaza II.'[100]

Incomplete Coordination, Unrealized Adjustment

By early 1987, the dollar had fallen approximately 36 percent against the mark and the yen since the Plaza accord, and 47 and 42 percent, respectively, from its late February 1985 peak. On an effective basis, the depreciation measured roughly one-third of its former value. However, current account imbalances continued to worsen in 1986 and while much of this was the result of temporary J-curve effects, most projections foresee large deficits for the United States and large surpluses for Japan and Germany continuing into the next decade.[101] (Some forecasts even predict that, at exchange rates prevailing in early 1987, after a few years of modest improvement the United States current deficit will worsen again!) Greater correction in exchange rates and policies will be necessary in order to bring about complete adjustment. A fundamental question is whether adjustment will win the race against trade protectionism and the domestic political forces of autarchy.

The 1984–86 period saw significant cooperation on monetary policy. Interest rates among the United States, Japan, and Europe were reduced substantially during 1986 and in early 1987. Monetary diplomacy among the G-5 was largely responsible for the joint easing of monetary policy and, thus, the maintenance of growth among these economies. Without interest rate reductions in Japan and Europe, it would have been very difficult to lower American interest rates and the value of the dollar simultaneously, without triggering a panic selling of the currency. In 1986, each of the major industrial countries faced low or negative inflation, declining oil prices, and faltering growth. Under these circumstances, the interests of states in monetary loosening were harmonious and not as conflicting as public haggling over interest rates made them appear. By Volcker's own account, international coordination explained the *timing* of American discount rate decreases, rather than the direction of change.[102] Stronger conflicts of national interest arose over the question of differential monetary easing to shift the international pattern of demand expansion, an area in which diplomacy met with more limited success. Joint interest rate decreases did more to sustain world growth than to correct the trilateral current account imbalances.

Of the policy adjustments that have been implemented, Japan has undertaken the greatest commitments of the three largest economies. Japan accelerated the internationalization of its capital markets under pressure from the Reagan administration. For a short period, the Bank of Japan tightened monetary policy substantially in order to accelerate yen appreciation. The Japanese cooperated with U.S. authorities for six months while the yen continued to appreciate quickly. Moreover, Japan has left the door open to consideration of significant increases in domestic demand, although it has made few specific commitments to follow through in the public sector.

The Japanese measures, though partial and halting, stand in

40

contrast to German and American contributions to policy co-ordination. The German stimulus in early l988 may not be fast enough to avert a further depreciation of the dollar against the mark. Rather than shrinking, the American federal budget deficit grew during 1986, and it appears unlikely that the Gramm-Rudman targets will be met for 1987 or 1988. None-theless, there will probably be very large reductions in the Amercian budget deficit over the next two years. The erosion of opposition to tax increases in the now firmly Democratic-controlled Congress may assist reduction of the budget deficit. But whether these reforms come sufficiently quickly and are adequately sustained is a moot point.

During most of this period, international conflicts over macroeconomic policies have not visibly damaged the domestic popularity of American, Japanese, or German governments. In Japan, the political fortunes of the LDP and the Prime Minister were never as good during the postwar period as they were in mid-1986. Despite some criticism for making concessions to the Americans, the Japanese public seemed broadly supportive of the government's program of administrative reform coupled with Nakasone's conciliatory assurances to foreigners. In Germany, the conservative-liberal coalition, as a whole, made a strong showing in the elections in early 1987. Despite significant support within the country for stimulating domestic demand, resistance to foreign pressure was a popular stance. Nor did President Reagan suffer from his unwillingness to reduce the budget deficit, by raising taxes if necessary, as some foreign heads of government advised. Instead, Reagan successfully circumvented the issue with tax reform, which the Japanese and Europeans are preparing to emulate. For the governments involved, the political lesson of the 1984–86 period is that it is better to urge partners to make adjustments than to undertake politically unpopular policy adjustments oneself, even if those partners refuse to accept such commitments and conflict remains unresolved.

This may well be different, however, in 1987 and 1988. Over the next two years, exchange rate pressures will subject the German and Japanese economies to adjustment, perhaps more severely than has been predicted in many of the econometric models. Indeed, in the fourth quarter of 1986, robust increases in domestic demand were entirely offset by reduction in the trade surplus in Germany. In Japan, the effects of yen appreciation on real growth and employment will probably be even more painful. The reduced contribution of foreign demand to national growth will very likely change the political calculus confronting policy makers on economic policy decisions. In the United States, improvements in the trade balance over the next two years may offer an opportunity to offset the restrictive effects of budget deficit consolidation. International policy coordination becomes a domestic issue only when the effects of conflict are felt domestically.

V
Explaining Macroeconomic Conflict and Cooperation

The G-5 governments faced a classic dilemma of collective action in generating world economic recovery in the mid-1980s. When the world recession bottomed out in 1982, the United States preferred to stimulate its economy, regardless of what the Europeans and Japanese chose to do. The relative closure of the U.S. economy caused this fundamental asymmetry in the strategic problems faced by the major advanced countries. The Europeans and Japanese could not have pulled the United States out of its recession — although they may have been able to ameliorate it — and could have slowed the U.S. recovery only partially by not reflating. In contrast, U.S. reflation has had a large impact on its partners' economies.[103]

The Background to Conflict

U.S. domestic politics explain the American choice of monetary and fiscal policies, which induced high interest rates and provoked complaints from the rest of the world. The overriding economic priority of the first Reagan administration was not foreign concerns but its domestic program of tax cuts, expenditure reductions in domestic programs, the maintenance of non-inflationary monetary policy and regulatory reform. The initial political strategy for the administration's fiscal proposals was first to reduce taxes, and then to demand a reduction in domestic spending. Tax increases of sufficient magnitude to halt the upward trend in deficits were specifically ruled out by the President. With the deficits as a key part of the administration's strategy to get Congress to reduce spending, Reagan was not about to accommodate the international outcry from conservatives and socialists alike against the American budget deficits. And with fiscal policy captive to political strategies, monetary policy had to be targeted toward reducing inflation. International macroeconomic conflict was the external manifestation of the administration's choice of strategy in its domestic political engagement.

By 1984, economic conditions had changed the desired policy goals for the United States. American fiscal policy had delivered its stimulus and the domestic consensus was that it should be restricted, if politically possible. Further, the current account deficit had already reached record proportions, and the consensus was that it, too, should be reduced. Americans, thus, preferred that Germany and Japan adopt more expansionary fiscal policies, and the United States reduce its budget and current account deficits. A reflationary dilemma of collective action confronted the G-5 at this point. The resulting international conflict was the consequence of opposing interests over which countries should stimulate demand in which all would, to some extent, share.

The Outcome of Conflict

It is clear that domestic political divisions have not generated at any time during the 1980s policy coordination on the scale of the Bonn summit of 1978, despite the prevalence of strong divisions over macroeconomic policy issues within all governments at various points. It is clear that these internal divisions are not a sufficient condition for international coordination. In 1978, both Carter and Schmidt allowed themselves to be swayed by the shifting preferences of cabinet and coalition members. During the 1980s, in contrast, Reagan, Thatcher and Kohl displayed little willingness to entertain suggestions for basic policy changes. The adamant attitude of the American President against tax increases effectively discouraged his aides from intimating to foreign officials that pressure from abroad for tax increases might be helpful. The conclusion of earlier studies that unified governments are *not* a necessary condition for meaningful cooperation is now important, as there are divisions within each of the G-5 governments and key factions support cooperative policies.

The ability of countries to pursue independent macro-economic policies and induce others to change theirs — macro-economic power — explains important aspects of the outcome of macroeconomic conflict in the 1980s. During 1981–83 capital movements out of Europe and Japan toward the United States reinforced the administration's goal of reducing world-wide inflation. European governments wanting to moderate the depreciation of their currencies had strong incentives to adopt more restrictive monetary policies.[104] To the extent that they permitted depreciation, externally induced growth and inflation allowed for tighter policies within these countries. In this way, American policy operated through markets to alter the incentives faced by other governments, in such a way as to nudge these countries toward replicating the U.S. demand policy stance.[105]

France felt these effects most strongly during 1981–83. While the French had little difficulty in arranging official financing during this period, the amounts they had to raise were reduced by their previous imposition of capital and exchange controls to stem the outflow of private capital. With unchanged macroeconomic policies, the government could only look forward to a burgeoning foreign debt burden. This, in addition to three successive devaluations of the franc within the EMS, became an important domestic political issue. Given these projected costs of adhering to his Keynesian policy course, Mitterrand changed the thrust of his macroeconomic program.[106] While the unwillingness of the Reagan administration to help ease international constraints on French policy contributed to this change, American policies were not the only source of external limitations on France. The policies of Britain and Germany, and Mitterrand's decision to remain within the EMS, also imposed similar constraints independent of American policies.

During 1985 and 1986, exchange rate changes also favored the United States in policy conflict. Whereas the earlier appreciation of the dollar reduced American price increases at a time when world inflation was high, the depreciation of the dollar came at a time when world prices were weak — a very favorable time distribution.[107] The Europeans and Japanese, on the other hand, risked a greater inflation when their underlying domestically generated rates were high, and then saw their inflation rates reduced by currency appreciation vis-à-vis the dollar when inflation had already been largely conquered — an unfavorable pattern. These external price developments argued for restraint of European demand in the earlier period and expansion in the later period. But these incentives were clearly insufficient to induce Germany and Japan to expand domestic demand substantially in 1984–86. The greater sensitivity of their economies to exchange rate changes, however, does explain why, in a low-inflation environment, Germany and Japan cooperated, albeit partially and grudgingly, in joint interest rate reductions with the United States.

The differing responses of Japan and Germany to American pressure can be explained by trade power. Japan relies on the U.S. market for a significantly larger share of its exports — representing a larger share of GDP — than does Germany, France or Britain (see Table 5). Accordingly, American threats of market closure are more effective in eliciting a conciliatory Japanese response than a German one. Both administration officials and members of Congress explicitly linked U.S. trade policy to Japanese macroeconomic and trade policies during 1984–86. Accordingly, Japanese cooperation on monetary and exchange rate policies with the United States, while by no means resolving conflict, has been greater than German cooperation to date.

In summary, American power contributed to the general shift of demand policies toward deflation and to the ability of the United States to avoid adjusting its policy mix in 1981–83.[108] It can also account for the variation in outcome of relations between the United States and France in 1981–83, the United States and Japan in 1984–86, and the United States and

TABLE 5:
EXPORTS TO THE UNITED STATES FROM JAPAN, GERMANY, FRANCE AND THE UNITED KINGDOM, 1984

	Exports to United States by value (billions of $)	As percentage of total exports	As percentage of of GDP
Japan	60.4	35.6	4.9
Germany	17.8	10.4	2.9
France	8.5	8.8	1.8
United Kingdom	15.0	16.0	3.5

Source: IMF, *Direction of Trade Statistics.*

46

Germany in 1984–86; and for limited monetary cooperation in 1986. The American macroeconomic power has *not* been sufficient to induce the Japanese and Germans to provide more than marginal fiscal stimuli to domestic demand in 1984–86. However, we may not have yet observed the full effects of American influence on German and Japanese fiscal policy through the exchange rate, as of early 1987.

What explains the different overall potency of American power between the two periods? First, during the early 1980s, the United States sought mainly to deflect adjustment. It was not yet suffering severe balance-of-payments problems, and tried to induce its partners, primarily France, to undertake fundamental change in macroeconomic policy. In the latter period, the United States urged affirmative adjustment on other countries whose economies were also considerably larger than the French economy. There is, thus, an apparent asymmetry in the effectiveness of U.S. power between inducing adjustment on the part of others and deflecting others' attempts to influence American policy. Second, resistance to stimulating domestic demand on the part of important groups, parties, and, in particular, ministries in Germany and Japan, was stronger than resistance to deflationary policies in 1981–83. Domestic politics, indeed, impeded the translation of changes in macroeconomic opportunity cost into changes in policy in 1984–86. On the other hand, American trade politics was partly responsible for giving greater multilateralism to U.S. monetary and exchange rate policies. And it is still possible that this round of policy conflict will be concluded by an international agreement that links common domestic interests in macroeconomic coordination.

Learning Cooperation: Domestic Politics and Foreign Economic Policy

In the present world economic environment, uncertainty prevails. States cannot anticipate economic events, predict the consequences of macroeconomic conflict, or accurately measure the benefits of coordination with a high level of confidence. As national interests are often ambiguous, government leaders are less independent from group and constituency politics. The way states interpret past experience and use information is important for a more complete understanding of macroeconomic diplomacy under these circumstances. Learning and domestic politics can help to explain outcomes which seem to defy power.

To be useful, the concept of learning must extent beyond the simple adaptation to changing circumstances. Ernst Haas has defined it as 'the ability and willingness on the part of the relevant actors to incorporate consensual knowledge into the definition of interests that motivate international behavior.'[109] This kind of learning develops skill or knowledge leading to redefinition of national interests or greater effectiveness in achieving objectives. In economic affairs, states draw lessons from experience for macroeconomics and policy coordination. As incorporated into collective wisdom, these lessons have not been, and are not likely to be, sophisticated. While economists carefully separate causal linkages and differentiate between episodes, the general public and politicians do not make such fine distinctions. Instead, they tend to recommend measures that seemed to work in the most recent, comparable situation and avoid those that did not succeed, with little ability to distinguish between the effects of state policies and the effects of non-policy events on economic outcomes. Nye cautions, therefore, that lessons from past experience can be perverse, 'negative learning.'[110] Particular 'lessons' can lead countries to act less effectively than if they followed other interpretations of the past.

Fortunately, despite the complexity of macroeconomics, very simple lessons should be sufficient for progress in international policy coordination. Recognition of the openness of national economies, the costs of sustained currency misalignments and policy conflict, and the necessity for adjustment, eventually should move governments toward serious bargaining on macroeconomic positions. There have been serious flaws in the learning processes in the United States, Germany, and Japan, which are related to domestic politics. One of the functions that an international macroeconomic regime should serve is to encourage positive and discourage negative learning.

The United States

The Carter administration learned relatively quickly that it could not reflate irrespective of others' macroeconomic policies: both monetary and fiscal policies were tightened during 1978–

48

79. After the adjustments made with the dollar rescue package in November 1978, the United States continued an active foreign exchange policy. These were positive developments. But with the change in administration in 1981, this experience seems to have been lost; the learning which had taken place was not broad enough to survive the change in administration. The process had to begin anew in 1981.[111]

American international economic policy indeed underwent remarkable changes during the two controversies in the 1980s. While the Reagan administration held strong views about what foreign monetary and fiscal policies should be, those views were not pushed as strongly on foreign governments during 1981–83 as during 1984–86. In the earlier period, U.S. officials were content to let foreign countries shoulder the costs of taking a different policy route from the Reagan program, as long as the United States was not expected to amend policies to make others' choices easier for them. The second Reagan administration, in contrast, strongly pressured foreign governments to reflate their economies and appreciate their currencies; it was more successful in the latter than in the former. The Treasury and the Fed promoted cooperative reductions in interest rates among the G-5 countries. Moreover, Treasury officials sought to strengthen the process of multilateral surveillance, while making no commitments on American policy adjustment. Whereas the first Reagan administration was openly suspicious of coordination as a ploy to water down Reaganomics, the second administration trumpeted it as a keystone to world economic management. No longer could governments best serve the world economy by best serving themselves.

By mid-1986, the change in Reagan administration outlook on international coordination had become total. Secretary Baker's statements seemed to place him among the most ardent of trilateralists:

More and more, governments today realize that to a great extent their own domestic prosperity hinges on the condition of the international economy . . . .

The great interdependence of nations that resulted from the expansion of an open system of trade and payments has, almost by definition, increased each country's vulnerability to developments in other nations. Unfortunately, the evolution of our arrangements for cooperation among nations has not

49

kept pace with the requirements of growing interdependence. Perhaps most importantly, political institutions have not fully adapted to that reality.

For the United States ... the time is long past when the United States could, in setting domestic policies, relegate external considerations to a second order of importance.

The experience of the interwar period convinced one generation that the only acceptable answer lay in greater cooperation. I am confident that the present generation need not relive history to absorb its lessons. To extend the framework of international economic cooperation will not be easy, but it is the only responsible course.[112]

Speaking before the World Bank and IMF 1986 annual meeting, President Reagan himself extolled the postwar international 'economic constitution' that these institutions, with GATT, represented, and the prosperity that they helped to generate. Moreover, he argued that the passing of 'America's singular strength' necessitated 'strong and growing roles' for them.[113] To what extent does this change in American international economic policy represent positive learning or the mere adaptation to changing and reversible circumstances?

As world economic conditions evolved, the administration's main foreign economic objectives shifted from protecting the domestic program and reducing inflation abroad to maintaining the world and U.S. recovery by stimulating foreign demand. During the first phase, the administration could achieve what it wanted by unilaterally pursuing its own domestic objectives. Indeed, far from constraining U.S. economic performance, the world economy supported domestic investment and helped reduce the rate of inflation by massive capital inflows and an appreciating dollar. Two changes altered American objectives during the second phase. First, the American authorities had exhausted the stimulative potential of fiscal policy and, largely, of monetary policy. Second, the current account deficit had become unsustainably large, and the United States was dependent on the continued *ex ante* flow of capital to hold American interest rates low. To avoid the economic and political costs of adjustment, the administration sought adjustment on the part of the Europeans and Japanese.

The experiences of the Carter and Reagan administrations are fairly typical of the pattern of change in U.S. policy since the

50

1960s. When current account deficits become unsustainable, international economic factors will be taken into consideration in U.S. foreign economic policy, and perhaps in monetary and fiscal policy as well. When these deficits are manageable, domestic politics will direct economic policy to a greater extent. Consequently, the United States pursues multilateral strategies when foreign economic performance is a proximate constraint on American prosperity and more unilateral strategies when it is not. The incorporation of international considerations into American policy-making varies considerably over time.

These observations help us to build a simple, dynamic model of U.S. international monetary and macroeconomic policy, driven by shifting balances of external and domestic influences on policy.[114] U.S. policy tends to pass through three sequential stages. First, economic policy is made with domestic considerations foremost. Foreign economic policy is generally designed to serve the domestic program. During the past two decades, this period of domestic primacy coincided with new administrations coming to Washington, generally not cognizant of the external effects of domestic policies. Consequently, the trade and current account deficits grew toward unsustainable levels, creating future constraints on American policies.

Second, once international markets inevitably make the U.S. government aware of external constraints, American officials attempt initially to induce others to bear the full costs of adjustment. They rely on American power resources in doing so, in particular greater American willingness to countenance large swings in exchange rates. But, as American power is insufficient to persuade foreign governments to bear all of the costs of adjustment — as the 1977–78 and the 1984–86 experiences demonstrate — officials will search for new strategies.

The third, and last phase, is characterized by serious negotiating and bargaining with foreign governments over the distribution of the costs of adjustment. American officials continue to exercise power, but do not rely exclusively on it. Success will also depend on bargaining skills and entrepreneurial negotiating. Bargaining may be hard and threats exchanged, but negotiating will be serious and directed toward an agreement in which adjustment is largely mutual, though not necessarily perfectly balanced.

These three phases of international monetary and macroeconomic policy — neglect, conflict, and mutual adjustment —

are sequential. American administrations tend to pass through each: first, seemingly unaware of potential external constraints; then, once aware of them, attempting to induce others to bear the costs of adjustment; and, finally, compromising on the distribution of the costs of adjustment. Governments tend not to enter into compromises without first trying to deflect adjustment burdens. Some administrations may pass through these stages more quickly than others but they pass through each stage in sequence.[115] (During the six years under Reagan, the administration appears to be approaching the end of the second stage). Once an administration has adopted a cooperative strategy, it tends not to revert back to earlier unilateral and aggressive tactics. However, domestic politics will inevitably bring a change of administration which will start the cycle anew.[116] In the United States, learning is not broad enough to encompass incoming as well as outgoing officials.

The unsustainability of the current account balance and value of the dollar is a key feature of this cycle.[117] In early 1985, the President himself referred to the current account deficit as 'unsustainable,' but the economic logic of this realization had not permeated policy sufficiently to prevent him from extolling the United States, in almost the same breath, as the 'investment capital of the world.'[118] It took the serious prospect of losing control over trade policy to an angry Congress to motivate the administration to take positive efforts to guide the dollar to lower, more reasonable levels.[119] The Treasury was also motivated to depreciate the dollar and improve exchange arrangements by efforts made by members of Congress to restrict severely the Treasurer's discretion in that area.[120] The learning cycle of neglect, conflict, and cooperation is a function of the interplay of international and domestic politics.

To the administration's credit, lay officials are now more cognizant of the external effects of U.S. policy and foreign constraints on it. Increased awareness also extends to members of Congress. It is impossible to know at this time, however, whether this awareness represents hard-won lessons or mere adaptation to changing circumstances. The key test will come when the balance of payments constraint on U.S. monetary and fiscal policies loosens and protectionism abates.

52

Germany and Japan also demonstrate cycles of relative sensitivity and insensitivity to the external effects of their macroeconomic policies. Each has pursued its very successful postwar economic strategy within the framework of liberal international economic regimes with, at times, little explicit attention to the costs it might be imposing on the system and its partners — what Cooper describes as a 'small country perspective.'[121] When partners' objections become so strong as to threaten the open system of trade and finance, and perhaps foreign and security ties as well, German and Japanese governments will accede to amicable compromises reflecting a broader perspective, but often not before conflicts have become serious. Although Germany's prominent role in the EC sharply differentiates it from Japan, the two countries have been broadly similar in this respect.

While generally more aware of the effects of the exchange rate on their economies, Germany and Japan seem to have learned little more than the United States about external constraints and the inevitability of adjustment. Indeed, while the United States' positive learning experience of the late 1970s was lost to a change in government in 1981, Germany and Japan seem to have actually drawn negative lessons from the same experience. The received wisdom in Germany has been particularly averse to international coordination. Coordination became guilty by association with the high inflation, current account deficits, and the high levels of government debt that confronted Germany at the outset of the 1980s (notwithstanding considerable uncertainty over the strength of the causal link to the measures agreed to at the Bonn summit in 1978). For domestic political reasons, that indictment was later delivered by many of the same officials who had earlier determined that coordination was in Germany's national interest.

In 1978, the important German economic officials, political parties and interest groups virtually unanimously supported the Chancellor's decision at the summit in Bonn to agree to a fiscal stimulus equivalent to one percent of GNP.[122] However, public myth, inside and outside Germany, currently holds that Bonn altruistically conceded to foreign pleas to buoy world economic growth by stimulating domestic demand.[123] The German measures were in fact no more altruistic than President Carter's agreement to decontrol American domestic oil prices. Indeed, some commentators argued at the time that the United States had accepted the greater burden at Bonn. The fact is that each leader believed that he was acting in his own country's interest when agreeing on new economic measures at the 1978 summit. How the misconception that the Germans were acting altruistically was able to become widespread is illustrated by Helmut Schmidt's domestic political strategy on fiscal issues. (Germany is used here only as an example, albeit a particularly good one, of the kind of backsliding that occurs in all countries). A master tactician, Schmidt sought to be 'pushed' by foreign leaders and domestic groups into taking the stimulus decision at Bonn, although he privately agreed that the stimulus would be in Germany's own interest. In order to extract an American *quid pro quo*, Schmidt's representation of the German stimulus as an international concession worked to his government's advantage. But, when confronted with domestic criticism on Germany's federal budget deficit in later years, he has used foreign pressure for the stimulus as an excuse, and has repeatedly disparaged the 'locomotive theory.'[124] Moreover, the fact that U.S. oil price decontrol and the successful conclusion of the Tokyo Round were also in Germany's interest has been largely ignored. Unless the public is informed through a more careful explication of coordination rationale, it will be difficult to argue, years later, that national measures were accompanied by beneficial foreign concessions as well. This negative lesson was inauspicious for German participation in trilateral macro-economic policy coordination in the 1980s.

The Japanese experienced high inflation, unprecedented current deficits, and disturbing levels of government debt in 1979–81. Further, the growth target agreed to by the then Prime Minister, Takeo Fukuda, became an issue during his replacement by Masayoshi Ohira. Nevertheless, the Japanese public seems less opposed than the Germans to the idea of international coordination, even when subjected to a great deal of foreign pressure. High levels of government debt are associated with pressure from Washington to stimulate domestic demand, and accounts for current resistance to deferring fiscal consolidation. While Japanese resentment of American pressure on economic issues appears to be increasing, foreign pressure does not seem to be actually counterproductive, as in Germany. There is a premium placed on smooth relations with allies, which accounts for the Japanese style of symbolic politics and conciliatory expressions of intent, exemplified in the Maekawa Report, and which perhaps contributes to greater willingness to adjust monetary policy.

Conclusions: Toward an International Macroeconomic Regime

International discussions to bring exchange rates to long-term equilibrium values and restore balance in international accounts will necessarily focus on macroeconomic policies. Notions and expectations regarding satisfactory collective and national growth, inflation, and unemployment will inevitably influence, if not dominate, the resolution of international monetary issues. For this reason, it is useful to broaden our conventional conception of the international monetary regime — concerned with exchange rates, international liquidity and finance, and balances of payments — to include the implicit and explicit rules, norms, and procedures governing negotiations and the establishment of agreements on macroeconomic policies. Enveloping the monetary regime, this broader concept could be called an *international macroeconomic regime.*[125] The macroeconomic regime would be explicitly cognizant of the macroeconomic performance and interdependence of states and how macroeconomics should condition adjustment obligations. In concept, the macroeconomic is distinguished from the monetary regime in that the sum of national macroeconomic performance objectives implies collective objectives as well. In practice, rules establishing national obligations regarding exchange rates cannot be applied without reference to the macroeconomic performance of member states, because international monetary objectives will usually be subordinate to the macroeconomic objectives of the large countries. The macroeconomic regime was very weak, at best, in the 1980s. This concluding section suggests how the multilateral surveillance process could be further enhanced and used to buttress exchange-rate stabilization regimes.

To strengthen the international macroeconomic regime, the

advanced countries would have to conclude an overarching accord that guides the making of specific macroeconomic policy bargains. The European and Japanese governments must pre-commit themselves to negotiating agreements on the level of domestic demand to sustain their own economies. The United States must forswear use of the exchange rate to capture a greater or lesser share of total world demand when foreign economic policies conflict with American preferences. This accord would require that national macroeconomic objectives do not diverge greatly and that the United States manages fiscal and monetary policy so as to maintain at least moderate growth and no more than moderate inflation. This is an agreement which has eluded the advanced countries, except for short periods, since the transformation of the Bretton Woods regime fifteen years ago. Despite imperfections in the exchange rate weapon, the United States has been unwilling to surrender this source of macroeconomic power without at least limited assurance that surplus countries would augment domestic demand when the United States faces both adjustment and weak world growth. Likewise, Europe and Japan have refused to offer such guarantees without American assurances of exchange rate stability and stable macroeconomic policies. Despite advantages over time for all countries in reaching this overarching accord, at each critical juncture at least one major government has preferred to preserve its prerogative to rely on foreign demand or to orchestrate currency appreciation or depreciation. The difficulty in concluding the bargain, then, is not simply that the benefits may not be recognized (though this is surely an important obstacle), but that it involves a sensitive trade-off: while in the long term the bargain is balanced, in the short term the sacrifices tend to be asymmetrical among deal-making governments. Asymmetrical sacrifices are especially difficult to justify to domestic constituencies and ministers who place a high value on future benefits emanating from an accord.

Regime Alternatives

The machinery of international cooperation will have to address problems at both the international and domestic levels. The international monetary regime will have to restrain states from proscribed behavior (for example, unwarranted manipulation of their currencies, accumulation of excess current account surpluses, and permitting excessive inflation) and facilitate the reaching of mutually beneficial agreements among them.[126] But, because domestic political imperatives have overpowered regime constraints and undermined agreements in the past, cooperation should also have a domestic component. A domestic component would serve to extinguish the cycles of neglect, conflict, and cooperation to some extent characteristic of all states by institutionalizing the regime in domestic policy-making procedures. In order to facilitate multilateral trade-offs, it will be particularly important to impress upon domestic policy makers and the public the future costs of unilateral policies and, in effect, to lower the discount rate applied to those costs. Domestic reforms could also contribute to cooperation through a long-term process of positive national learning, which international regimes can facilitate.[127] By building bridges between domestic policy-making processes and the international regime, we can improve the sensitivity of international agreements to domestic political imperatives and the receptivity of the domestic sphere to international agreements.

All proposals for reducing exchange rate fluctuations rely to some extent on macroeconomic policy coordination. The degree of coordination required varies inversely to the fixity of rates envisioned in the stabilization scheme. The specificity and clarity of the international macroeconomic regime and requisite domestic reforms rise with the coordination requirement. As the tightness of coordination increases, so does the frequency of international consultations, institutional support which consultations require, specificity of criteria for assigning adjustment responsibilities, precision of economic analysis, degree of consensus on implied collective performance, and the extent of precommitment to 'remedial action.'

Ad Hoc Cooperation

The loosest regime might ignore exchange rate changes until speculative bubbles emerged or current account imbalances became clearly unsustainable. Under such a regime, coordination might be necessary only infrequently and pursued only on an ad hoc basis. The lack of clear economic criteria for the sustainability of a current account imbalance and the relative

58

congressional tolerance of large U.S. trade deficits up until 1985 argue for such a loose, ad hoc system. It could, for example, head off instability in the dollar market such as that which occurred in late 1984 and early 1985, but it would require greater cooperation among the G-5 than we have seen during much of the 1980s.

Target Zones

A broad-banded target zone system would seek to avoid any substantial misalignment of exchange rates. Such a system would require a greater level of coordination than one designed to avoid sustained misalignment and speculative bubbles. As envisioned by John Williamson, if regular consultations could not resolve differences, negotiations over the modification of macroeconomic policies would be triggered by the exchange rate reaching the limits of the target zone.[128] Under this regime, coordination need not be continuous, but it would occur more frequently than on an ad hoc basis. Exchange rates would likely meander for a time within the zone before testing its boundaries, and might even be permitted to fluctuate outside the zone for a time, pending corrective action. Broad agreement on collective macroeconomic performance would be important, although there would be considerable room for national divergence. Monetary policy would be targeted mainly, though not exclusively, on the exchange rate. Fiscal policy would be directed toward internal balance and would have to be managed consistently with monetary policy constrained by the zones. But, especially under wide zones, fiscal policy would not necessarily have to be operated perfectly flexibly. Permitted exchange rate fluctuation within the zones could accommodate some inflexibility in the use of fiscal policy, although certainly not as much as characterized the 1980s. Broad zones, with perhaps 10 percent margins, would also accommodate imprecision in governments' ability to specify equilibrium exchange rates.

McKinnon's target zone proposal sees no need for fiscal coordination but makes strong demands on monetary coordination.[129] Under his scheme, the monetary base of the United States, Germany, and Japan would ultimately be *jointly* determined by the three central banks. First within broad and then within narrow zones, exchange rate changes would signal the need for deviations in national money supply growth from the prenegotiated, three-country average. For McKinnon, the integrity of the zone is more important, because he expects hard boundaries to stabilize market expectations. National monetary policies would have very little scope for domestic stabilization not part of the internationally negotiated accord. Despite these restraints, under all broad-banded versions of target zone systems, large current account imbalances might still emerge.

EMS-Type Coordination

Exchange rates among the dollar, yen, and mark might be linked together as tightly as the European currencies are under the EMS. Under the EMS, currencies fluctuate within bands of 2.25 percent on either side of their central parities (the Italian lira has 6 percent margins) but are adjusted occasionally to accommodate trend divergences in inflation and productivity. Operating this system in practice has required relatively tight coordination of monetary policy — with the German Bundesbank setting the pace — but which falls considerably short of McKinnon's joint policy. The EMS has seen less convergence of fiscal policy. Major fiscal divergences — such as the French expansion of 1981–83 — have been accommodated by realignments of central parities. Successfully operating this system requires frequent consultation among finance ministers and close operational coordination of monetary policy by central banks. Although, in practice, the European countries have never actually adopted collective targets, the EMS presupposes national performance objectives which are broadly consistent. On a world scale, tight currency bands would require an equivalent commitment to macroeconomic policy coordination among the United States, Japan, and Europe — a commitment made all the more problematic by the relative closure of these three economic blocks to one another, compared to the European countries, and by the absence of an institutional framework, such as the European Community, at the global level.

Overall Evaluation

The macroeconomic diplomatic experience of the 1980s offers

better prospects for a looser rather than a tighter macro-economic regime. An EMS-style exchange rate system would be too demanding of tripartite coordination at this point. Moreover, it would be unnecessary: the United States, Japan, and Europe could live quite comfortably with exchange rate changes much larger than those permitted by the EMS, provided fluctuations centered on equilibrium values. But a loose system that required ad hoc coordination or a target zone system needing occasional coordination would be useful and feasible with less radical reforms. More successful coordination of monetary compared to fiscal policy during the mid-1980s accords with the most basic requirement of a target zone system: that monetary policy take into account exchange rate considerations. The level of monetary cooperation demanded by the McKinnon proposal is, however, out of reach at present. The Federal Reserve and Bundesbank both vigilantly safeguard their independence from their respective governments, not to mention vis-à-vis foreign central banks. Even under the Williamson version, however, the inflexibility of fiscal policy during the 1980s would have to be changed. This would require formidable, though not impossible, reforms at the domestic level and a fairly concrete precommitment to objective indicators of macroeconomic performance. A looser system based on ad hoc coordination would avoid continuous bargaining over policies and might be lucky enough to avoid making changes in national fiscal policies, but at the cost of prolonging misalignments.

The multilateral surveillance process currently used by the G-5 meets the regime requirements of ad hoc coordination only in part. The regular meetings among finance ministers and central bankers provide a forum in which macroeconomic agreements can be reached, if the participants are so inclined. These meetings also enable each minister to understand better the domestic political calculus facing his counterparts. But the process as presently operated offers very few constraints of even the mildest form on state policies. The system of indicators offers no guidance for assigning adjustment responsibilities, but moderate compulsion could be introduced by the G-5 taking the indicators exercise seriously and slimming down the performance criteria used. The Group should specify a medium-term plan indicating growth and inflation goals. If exchange rates or current balances became unacceptable, adjustment could be assigned on the basis of whether growth in the OECD was above or below that envisioned in the medium term, to offer one criterion. Under this arrangement, surplus countries would be expected to expand domestic demand when growth was sluggish, while deficit countries would constrain demand when growth outpaced the rate sustainable in the medium term. Alternatively, adjustment responsibilities might be assigned on the basis of different criteria, such as world commodity prices. Failure to take action would violate an implicit (if not explicit) bargain. The damage to reputation, albeit a moderate inducement, would act as an incentive to comply. Having the heads of government endorse and reaffirm the medium-term objectives at the G-7 summit meetings would give the plan greater stature and raise the costs of shirking adjustment responsibilities.

At the domestic level, the multilateral surveillance process could be expanded beyond the narrow circle of officials doing their work in secrecy. The closed meetings of the G-5 finance ministers and central bankers and of the G-7 are very useful and should remain private. However, greater transparency of the process — even if only after G-5 decisions have been made — could broaden understanding and support for G-5 achievements among domestic organs, particularly budgetary authorities. Three domestic-level reforms could add domestic political impetus.

First, the trade legislation being considered by the U.S. Congress, as of this writing, contains provisions that would require the Secretary of the Treasury to report to congressional committees on international monetary policy twice each year.[130] His reports would specify what exchange rate would be consistent with the state of trade and current account balances, the effects on production, employment and competitiveness of exchange rate misalignments, the causes of misalignment, and contain recommendations for policy changes needed to attain a sustainable current account balance. In addition, the proposed legislation would require the Treasury to submit to Congress the documents originating out of Article IV bilateral consultations with the IMF and explain why IMF recommendations were implemented or ignored. These are creative proposals which would serve to put U.S. international monetary policy on written record and explicate its rationale.

Second, it has been suggested that IMF rules be amended to

permit the Managing Director to testify before Congress on the issues relating to the international monetary system and management of the world economy.[131] Greater involvement in domestic economic debates poses some political risks for the IMF, but would generally raise the level of discussion and highlight international influences on American macroeconomic performance.

Third, the fiscal policy-making process in all countries could be structured so as to focus attention on the external effects of fiscal policy. The U.S. Congress, for example, could require that the President and the Office of Management and Budget include such an analysis in their annual budget statement. The administration could be asked to state what it expects the effect of the proposed budget and deficit (or surplus) to be on the exchange rate, capital flows, trade balance, and foreign economic conditions, and through what mechanism (if any) these effects would be felt. It would be useful to draw the relationship between fiscal policy and external as well as internal balance, particularly as changes in budget deficits in the United States, Japan, and Europe, have been the primary sources of *ex ante* changes in savings-investment balances influencing exchange rates and current balances.

These suggestions apply to the parallel policy-making processes in the other member countries of the G-5 as well. Highlighting the exchange rate-current balance relationship, opening up government-IMF consultations to public purview, and analyzing the external effects of both fiscal and monetary policies could improve the domestic conditions for international coordination. Despite the greater sensitivity of the German and Japanese economies to exchange rate changes, and to the larger external effects of changes in their domestic policies, formal and public studies of these effects are no more a part of German and Japanese fiscal and monetary policy-making processes than of American procedures. Although these policy-making processes differ substantially among the G-5, the basic principle behind these proposed reforms can also be applied to each of these national systems.

Naturally, putting these advisory reforms in place in the major advanced countries will not ensure that they actually generate international cooperation. Indeed, the economic analysis of the international effects of fiscal and monetary policy is controversial, with competing schools of thought. No law will

63

ensure that authorities actually make monetary and fiscal policies on the basis of exchange rate and current balance considerations. Experience shows that governments are often divided on the macroeconomic questions concerning international cooperation. Once in place, these measures could be used by those within governments in favor of coordinated outcomes, while they would tend to work to the disadvantage of factions advocating unilateralist policies. They could also discourage the practice of placing the blame for policy failures on the actions of other governments; when international packages are defended domestically as advancing the national interest, as they must be, government officials could not later claim to have succumbed to foreign pressure for altruistic concessions.

Perhaps most importantly, as analysis and evidence generated by these reporting provisions accumulates over time, and as countries gain experience with international macroeconomic bargaining, these changes could help to set in motion a long-term process of learning which causes countries to refine their notion of national interest in macroeconomic and monetary affairs. Changes in domestic and international policy processes of macroeconomic deliberations could make national learning cumulative. No international regime alone will be able to fully extinguish cycles of neglect, conflict, and cooperation. Coupled with complementary changes in domestic procedures, however, a macroeconomic regime could help positive learning survive changes in government, thereby taking macroeconomically interdependent countries off the merry-go-round of discord and placing them on an upward-sloping curve of enlightened, self-interested cooperation.

Notes

1. Robert O. Keohane, *After Hegemony: Cooperation and Discord in the World Political Economy* (Princeton: Princeton University Press, 1984), 53.
2. Stanley Hoffmann, 'Domestic Politics and Interdependence,' in *From Marshall Plan to Global Interdependence,* OECD (Paris, 1978), 183.
3. *Wall Street Journal Europe,* 2 October 1986.
4. Robert D. Putnam and C. Randall Henning, *The Bonn Economic Summit Meeting of 1978: How Does International Economic Policy Coordination Actually Work?* Brookings Discussion Papers in International Economics,

no. 53 (Washington, D.C., 16 April 1985). Henning, *The Politics of Macroeconomic Conflict and Coordination among Advanced Capitalist States, 1975–1985,* PhD dissertation, The Fletcher School of Law and Diplomacy, Tufts University, April 1985. Robert D. Putnam and Nicolas Bayne, *Hanging Together: The Seven-Power Summits* (Cambridge, MA: Harvard University Press, 1984) (hereafter cited as: Putnam and Bayne, *Hanging Together*). Dieter Hiss, 'Weltwirtschaftsgipfel: Betrachtungen eines Insiders' (World Economic Summit: Observations of an Insider), in *Empirische Wirtschaftsforschung,* ed. Jochim Frohn and Reiner Staeglin (Berlin: Duncker and Humbolt, 1980), 279–80, 282–4, and 286–7.

5. Putnam and Henning, *The Bonn Economic Summit Meeting of 1978,* 139--40. For an example of work that implies that domestic unity is a necessary condition for cooperation, see, Michael Artis and Sylvia Ostry, *International Economic Policy Coordination,* Chatham House Papers, no. 30 (London: Royal Institute of International Affairs, 1986), 75–6.

6. Hiss, 'Weltwirtschaftsgipfel,' in *Empirische Wirtschaftsforschung,* 286–7.

7. Putnam has elaborated on the interaction between the domestic and international levels with his 'Theory of Ratification,' in 'The Logic of Two-level Games: International Cooperation, Domestic Politics, and Western Summitry, 1975–1986,' paper delivered to the American Political Science Association annual meeting, Washington, D.C., 28–31 August 1986.

8. For an elaboration on power in macroeconomic relations, see, Henning, *The Politics of Macroeconomic Policy Conflict and Coordination among Advanced Capitalist States,* chap. 4.

9. The 'hegemonic stability thesis,' developed by Charles Kindleberger and Robert Gilpin, among others, is restated and examined in Keohane, *After Hegemony: Cooperation and Discord in the World Political Economy,* chap. 3. See, as well, the works reproduced in Robert O. Keohane, ed., *Neorealism and its Critics* (New York: Columbia University Press, 1986).

10. Two studies focusing on the role of power in macroeconomic conflict are, Robert O. Keohane, 'U.S. Foreign Economic Policy Toward Other Advanced Capitalist States: The Struggle to Make Others Adjust,' in *Eagle Entangled: U.S. Foreign Policy in a Complex World,* ed. Kenneth A. Oye, Donald Rothchild and Robert J. Lieber (New York: Longman, 1979), 91–122, especially 102–9, 118; Henry R. Nau, *International Reaganomics: A Domestic Approach to World Economy,* Center for Strategic and International Studies, Significant Issues Series, 6, no. 18 (Washington, D.C., 1984). Keohane argues that U.S. power was insufficient to induce others to adjust in the mid-1970s; Nau argues that because the Reagan administration sought to reduce inflation, open markets, and strengthen market incentives, the United States was successful in the early 1980s.

11. This body of literature is well developed. For a recent summary, see, Richard N. Cooper, 'Economic Interdependence and Coordination of Economic Policies,' in *Handbook in International Economics,* ed. Ronald Jones and Peter B. Kenen (Amsterdam: North-Holland, 1985). For recent contributions, see, Koichi Hamada, *The Political Economy of International Monetary Interdependence,* translated by Charles Yuji Horioka and Chi-Hung Kwan (Cambridge, MA: MIT Press, 1985); Willem H. Buiter and Richard C. Marston, eds., *International Economic Policy Coordination* (Cambridge: Cambridge University Press, 1985).

12. International economists also tend to believe that agreement on analytical frameworks (Keynesianism versus monetarism, for example) and macroeconomic objectives is a necessary condition for coordination. Indeed, differences among governments regarding analytical macroeconomic frameworks and values were strong during the 1980s. However, I will not treat them in depth here because I do not believe that they explain either the

65

pattern of cleavages among states on macroeconomic issues or the changes in policy that took place. When asked whether the Plaza accord reflected a convergence of views on the underlying analytical questions, one participant in the negotiations leading up to that agreement responded, 'No, we just agreed not to let those differences get in the way.'

The link between economic ideas and coordination is more complex than consensus on the former determining the latter. To achieve ongoing, continuous coordination — such as that envisioned by some in the multilateral surveillance system of objective indicators — analytical agreement may be a necessary precondition. Policy exchanges under this regime would be intertemporal. The burden of adjustment may be spread evenly over time, but at any one point asymmetrical sacrifices are likely to be required. Under these circumstances, agreement on analytical questions may be necessary to justify and legitimize one-sided policy changes. But, agreement on analytical frameworks is not necessary for *ad hoc*, occasional macroeconomic policy coordination, where mutual adjustments are negotiated.

Differences over analysis may be a contributing cause of conflict, but can be surmounted in conflict resolution and, in fact, these differences can also help states overlook conflicts of objective interests. See, Henning, *The Politics of Macroeconomic Conflict and Coordination*, chap. 8.

However, agreement on frameworks may well contribute to cooperation by clarifying the costs of macroeconomic conflict, and mutual awareness of one another's differing frameworks may make partners' policies more predictable. In this way, convergence of analytical views may alter governments' choices between power and bargaining strategies. The area is well worth future research; the present paper's space limitations prevent it from being addressed here.

For work attaching primary importance to analytical agreement, see, Richard N. Cooper, *International Cooperation in Public Health as a Prologue to Macroeconomic Cooperation*, Brookings Discussion Papers in International Economics, no. 44 (Washington, D.C., March 1986); Stephen N. Marris, *Managing the World Economy: Will We Ever Learn?* Essays in International Finance, no. 155 (Princeton: International Finance Section, October 1984); Marina v.N. Whitman, 'The Locomotive Approach to Sustaining World Recovery: Has It Run Out of Steam?' in *Contemporary Economic Problems, 1978*, ed. William Fellner (Washington, D.C.: American Enterprise Institute, 1978), 269–72. See, also, John S. Odell, *U.S. International Monetary Policy: Markets, Power and Ideas as Sources of Change* (Princeton: Princeton University Press, 1982); Jeffrey A. Frankel, *International Macroeconomic Policy Coordination When Policy-Makers Disagree on the Model*, National Bureau of Economic Research Working Paper no. 2059 (Cambridge, MA, October 1986).

13. Two exceptions are: Cooper, 'Economic Interdependence,' in *Handbook in International Economics*, and Gilles Oudiz and Jeffrey Sachs, 'Macroeconomic Policy Coordination among the Industrial Economies,' paper presented to the Brookings Panel on Economic Activity, Washington, D.C., 5–6 April 1984.

14. David D. Hale, 'World's Largest Debtor: The Risks of America's New Role as Capital Importer,' *Policy Review*, 38 (Fall 1986): 29.

15. Measured by the GNP deflator. As measured by the consumer price index, inflation for the OECD area was 12.9 percent in 1980. OECD, *Economic Outlook*, 30 (December 1981): 49 and 47 (Tables 24 and 22, respectively).

16. See, for example, the communiqué of the Venice summit, paragraph four, as published in *New York Times*, 24 June 1980.

17. Figures from OECD, *Economic Outlook*, 37 (Paris, June 1985): 157, 167, 165 (Tables R2, R12, R10, respectively).

18. OECD, *Economic Outlook*, 35 (Paris, July 1984): 24–39.
19. From 1982 to 1985, domestic demand in the United States rose by a full 18 percent, while Japanese domestic demand rose 9 percent and European demand 5 percent. See, Stephen N. Marris, *Deficits and the Dollar: The World Economy at Risk*, Policy Analyses in International Economics, no. 14 (Washington, D.C.: Institute for International Economics, forthcoming), preface to the Japanese edition.
20. Paul A. Volcker, 'Statement before the Committee on Foreign Affairs of the U.S. House of Representatives,' Federal Reserve press release, 18 June 1986, 24.
21. Calculated as the obverse of the current balance, as listed in OECD, *Main Economic Indicators* 86/6 (June 1986). EC, *European Economy*, 26 (November 1985): 177 (Table 34), estimates even more dramatic flows: U.S. 3.5; Japan -3.6; Germany -2.1; and the EC -0.5 percent of GDP, in 1985.
22. U.S. Council of Economic Advisers, *Annual Report, 1986* (Washington, D.C.: Government Printing Office, 1986), 339 (Table B-73).
23. Bank for International Settlements, various annual reports.
24. Bank for International Settlements, *Fifty-Sixth Annual Report* (Basle, June 1986), 44. The increase over previous years was due in large measure to increased Japanese direct purchases of U.S. Treasury securities and deposits in U.S. banks, and to a sizable increase in European purchases of U.S. corporate bonds.
25. Marris, *Deficits and the Dollar*, 45.
26. U.S. Council of Economic Advisers, *Annual Report, 1984* (Washington, D.C.: GPO, 1984), 55–7, 63–4. This report, prepared by former Chairman of the Council, Martin Feldstein, was disavowed by the White House and Treasury Secretary Donald Regan.
27. According to the IMF's multilateral exchange rate index, MERM. The index of the Federal Reserve shows a considerably greater appreciation of the dollar during this period.
28. John Williamson, *The Exchange Rate System*, Policy Analyses in International Economics, no. 5 (Washington, D.C.: Institute for International Economics, revised in June 1985), 79 (Table 12).
29. See, for example, U.S. Council of Economic Advisers, *Annual Report, 1984*, 45.
30. The United States began the decade in a net creditor position of $106 billion, raised that to $147 billion in 1982, and then allowed it to deteriorate to a net debtor position of roughly $250 billion at the end of l986. See, U.S. Department of Commerce, *Survey of Current Business* (Washington, D.C., June 1986), 27–28 (Tables 1 and 2). Islam stresses, however, that on financial investment alone — abstracting from foreign direct investment — the United States has been a net debtor throughout the 1970s. See, Shafiqul Islam, *Foreign Debt of the United States and the Dollar*, Federal Reserve Bank of New York Research Paper, no. 8415 (New York, September 1984).
31. C. Fred Bergsten and Shafiqul Islam, *The United States as a Debtor Country* (Washington, D.C.: Institute for International Economics, forthcoming).
32. Marina v.N. Whitman, 'Coordination and Management of the International Economy: A Search for Organizing Principles,' in *Reflections of Interdependence: Issues for Economic Theory and U.S. Policy* (Pittsburgh: University of Pittsburgh Press, 1979), 284. In this respect, macroeconomic conflict in the 1980s paralleled that in 1977–78; though increased capital mobility made conflicts of interest sharper in the later period.
33. For other accounts of international economic diplomacy of the 1980s, see:

Putnam and Bayne, *Hanging Together;* Nau, *International Reaganomics;* Benjamin J. Cohen, 'An Explosion in the Kitchen? Economic Relations with Other Advanced Industrial States,' in *Eagle Resurgent? The Reagan Era in American Foreign Policy*, ed. Kenneth Oye, Robert Lieber and Donald Rothchild (Boston: Little, Brown, 1987), 115–44 (hereafter cited as: Cohen, 'An Explosion in the Kitchen?'); and Artis and Ostry, *International Economic Policy Coordination*, 75–7.

34. See, for example, Otto Graf Lambsdorff, 'Reconciling Divergent Interests,' in *Economic Interests in the 1980's: Convergence or Divergence?*, ed. Gregory Flynn, Atlantic Papers no. 44–45 (Paris: Atlantic Institute for International Affairs, 1982), 9–22.

35. For a sympathetic account of the development and application of supply-side economics, see, Paul Craig Roberts, *The Supply-Side Revolution: An Insider's Account of Policymaking in Washington* (Cambridge, MA: Harvard University Press, 1984). See, as well, David A. Stockman, *The Triumph of Politics: Why the Reagan Revolution Failed* (New York: Harper and Row, 1986).

36. *International Herald Tribune*, 13 September 1982.

37. OECD, *Economic Outlook*, 34 (Paris, December 1983): 32–43.

38. *Financial Times*, 21 April 1981.

39. As Henry Nau coined the term, 'domesticism' is a strategy which plays down the role of international institutions and bargaining in favor of the 'use of vigorous national action, working indirectly through the international marketplace, to induce mutual adjustment of national policies toward low inflation, strong market incentives, and open borders.' See, Nau, 'Where Reaganomics Works,' *Foreign Policy*, 57 (Winter 1984–1985: 20–2.

40. *Financial Times*, 18 April 1981. At the outset of the Carter administration, too, the United States announced that it was agnostic with respect to the exchange rate. But, while reluctant to intervene, the Carter administration did not openly declare that it would not do so. See, U.S. Council of Economic Advisers, *Annual Report, 1978*, 124. When Treasury Secretary Blumenthal observed that markets would put upward pressure on the currencies of current account surplus countries, he was widely condemned for 'talking down the dollar.'

41. U.S. Congress, Joint Economic Committee, *International Economic Policy*, Hearings, 97th Cong., 1st sess., 4 May 1981. (During questioning, Congressman Henry Reuss asked Dr. Sprinkel whether the administration would want to intervene in the event that the new policies resulted in large budget deficits which, in combination with tight monetary policy, caused high interest rates, capital inflow and an appreciating dollar. Sprinkel answered that it would be doubtful, and challenged the premise of the question).

42. *New York Times*, 21 and 22 July 1981.

43. *Wall Street Journal* and *Washington Post*, 30 September 1981.

44. Joint Economic Committee *International Economic Policy*, 3.

45. Stephen Marris has pointed out that the doctrine of convergence is inconsistent with the administration's theory of flexible exchange rates. See, Marris, *Managing the World Economy: Will We Ever Learn?* Flexible rates were touted by their original proponents as enabling independent determination of the national price level. That the administration, nonetheless, adopted the convergence idea reflects the unwillingness of the Europeans to let exchange rates fluctuate freely and the inability of the Treasury to ignore the ensuing political problems.

46. *International Herald Tribune*, 18 May 1982.

47. *International Herald Tribune*, 2 March 1982; see, also, 26 April 1982.

48. The monetary agreement was tied to an agreement on East-West trade controls and credits. For the full story of the breakdown of the accord and the bitter exchanges that followed, see, Putnam and Bayne, *Hanging Together*, chap. 10.
49. Putnam and Bayne, *Hanging Together*, 185.
50. See excerpts from the intervention study reproduced in, Federal Reserve Bank of New York, *Quarterly Review*, 8 (Autumn 1983): 49. Only the conclusions of the study have been published as a joint document. Individual countries were given the option of publishing the research to which they had contributed. Several of the American papers were published as *Federal Reserve Staff Studies*, nos. 126–135 (September 1983–April 1985).
51. *New York Times*, 31 May 1983.
52. OECD, *Economic Outlook*, 35 (Paris, July 1984): 28 (Table 8).
53. *New York Times*, 11 July 1983.
54. Herbert Stein, *Presidential Economics: The Making of Economic Policy from Roosevelt to Reagan and Beyond* (New York: Simon and Schuster, 1984), 292.
55. *New York Times*, 11 October 1983.
56. See the communiqué, *New York Times*, 10 June 1984.
57. OECD, *Economic Surveys: United States* (Paris, November 1985).
58. *Wall Street Journal*, 13 November 1984.
59. *Wall Street Journal*, 10 December 1984.
60. This more affirmative approach was apparently raised by the National Security Adviser, Robert McFarlane and discussed at the White House shortly after the election. *Wall Street Journal*, 15 November 1986.
61. Eric Willenz, 'Why Europe Needs the Welfare State,' *Foreign Policy*, 63 (Summer 1986): 88–107.
62. Real short-term interest rates were about equal in the United States and Japan during 1983. See, Shafiqul Islam, 'Currency Misalignments: The Case of the Dollar and the Yen,' Federal Reserve Bank of New York, *Quarterly Review* (Winter 1983–84), 59, chart 3.
63. *Oriental Economist*, June 1984: 22–3, and July 1984: 18–32; Jeffrey A. Frankel, *The Yen/Dollar Agreement: Liberalizing Japanese Capital Markets*, Policy Analyses in International Economics, no. 9 (Washington, D.C.: Institute for International Economics, December 1984). Regan and Sprinkel believed that capital market liberalization would raise the value of the yen through greater overall demand for the currency outside Japan. Japanese policy-makers, being less monetarist, expected that liberalization would generate capital outflows, depressing the yen, and encouraging exports. The Japanese were correct in the medium term. This appears to be a classic case where differences over analytical frameworks permitted an agreement that might not otherwise have been reached.
64. In form and in some matters of substance, the Regan-Takeshita agreement bears an interesting resemblance to the Strauss-Ushiba accord of January 1978.
65. *Financial Times*, 3 January 1985.
66. *New York Times*, 25 January and 3 March 1985.
67. OECD, *Economic Outlook*, 37 (Paris, June 1985): 96.
68. *New York Times*, 24 February 1985.
69. *Wall Street Journal*, 27 February 1986.
70. Volcker was an adherent to the view that the federal budget deficits put upward pressure on U.S. interest rates causing capital inflow, a highly valued dollar, and current account deficits, and had been expressing this position for some time. See, Paul Volcker, 'Facing Up to the Twin Deficits,' *Challenge* (March/April 1984): 4–10. Several officials within the

69

administration agreed. See, Martin Feldstein, 'American Economic Policy and the World Economy,' *Foreign Affairs*, 63, no. 5 (Summer 1985): 995–1008.

71. Federal Reserve Bank of New York, *Quarterly Review*, 10 (Summer 1985): 58–9.
72. When the heads of state and government of seven major industrial countries suggested at the 1983 Williamsburg summit that a review be conducted of the international monetary system, responsibility for the undertaking was vested in what has come to be known as the 'Group of 10.' At both ministerial and the deputy ministerial levels, the Group of 10 had been conducting studies and discussions of global economic issues for some twenty years. The Group had its origins in the establishment of the IMF's General Arrangements to Borrow (GAB) in 1962. Under the General Arrangements ten major industrial countries — Belgium, Canada, France, Germany, Italy, Japan, the Netherlands, Sweden, the United Kingdom, and the United States — agreed to make lines of credit available to the IMF in their own currencies to finance drawings by any of the ten countries. The Group of 10 is not part of the formal structure of the IMF, but it is linked informally with the IMF through the GAB and through the nature of the issues with which it deals, as well as through the critical role its members play in IMF policy decisions.
73. IMF, 'Report of the G-10 Deputies on the Functioning of the International Monetary System,' *IMF Survey*, (July 1985), 2–14. The United States reportedly persuaded others to overrule a French proposal to declare in the report that there was a 'serious misalignment' of current exchange rates. *Wall Street Journal*, 17 May 1985.
74. *Financial Times*, 18 April 1985; *Wall Street Journal*, 15 April 1985.
75. *Wall Street Journal*, 26 April 1986. John Claggett Danforth (Republican, Missouri) was the chairman of the Senate trade subcommittee; Lloyd Bentsen (Texas) was chairman of a Senate Democratic working group on trade. Together, they represented something of a bipartisan view on the importance of the value of the dollar to trade.
76. Committee on Banking, Finance and Urban Affairs, House of Representatives, *Competitive Exchange Rate Act of 1985*, report, 99th Cong., 1st sess., 20 December 1985.
77. For a survey of these estimates, see John Williamson, *The Exchange Rate System*, Policy Analyses in International Economics, no. 5 (Washington, D.C.: Institute for International Economics, revised edition June 1985). These estimates were made for the dollar rate prevailing during the fourth quarter of 1984, which roughly equaled rates in May and June 1985.
78. OECD, *Economic Outlook*, 37 (June 1985), xv. The models referred to are the Japanese EPA model, the Federal Reserve Multicountry model, and the OECD's INTERLINK model.
79. These fears were expressed from many quarters. For a range of views, see, *Brookings Papers on Economic Activity* 1:1985 (Washington, D.C.: The Brookings Institution, 1985): 199–262.
80. Bank for International Settlements, *Fifty-Fifth Annual Report* (Basel, June 1985), 7–9, 176–82.
81. *New York Times*, 10 February 1985. Secretary of State Shultz, prior to the Bonn summit, put forth a comprehensive package of measures that included a reduction in the U.S. budget deficit; European policies to 'reduce obstacles to change and innovation,' attract capital and stimulate domestic investment; and Japanese policies to 'reduce the impact of [Japan's] high rate of domestic savings on its trade surplus.' Secretary Shultz, *National Policies and Global Prosperity*, Current Policy, no. 684 (Washington, D.C.: State Department, 11 April 1985).

82. *Wall Street Journal,* 27 and 28 February 1985.
83. For accounts of the development of the Plaza Accord, see, *Wall Street Journal,* 23 September 1985; *Washington Post,* 24 September 1985.
84. U.S. Department of the Treasury, press release, Washington, D.C., 22 September 1985.
85. *Washington Post,* 24 September 1985.
86. *Wall Street Journal,* 8 and 9 October 1985. The Bundesbank confirmed that the Plaza meeting did not change German monetary policy in 1985 but that faster growth of the money stock was allowed in 1986. Deutsche Bundesbank, *Report for the Year 1985,* (Frankfurt), 34.
87. *Washington Post,* 20 November 1985.
88. For example, British Chancellor of the Exchequer Nigel Lawson and French Finance Minister Pierre Beregovoy both declared that the United States had 'a lot to do' in regard to reducing the budget deficit. *Wall Street Journal,* 24 September 1985.
89. *Washington Post,* 22 October 1985.
90. *Wall Street Journal,* 6 June 1986.
91. *Economic Bulletin,* 22 (Cologne: German Institute for Economic Research, June 1985); *Financial Times,* 22 October 1986.
92. *New York Times,* 26 April 1986. Domestic political developments in both Germany and Japan during 1985–86 have very interesting parallels to the 1977–78 episode. In both periods, important groups and ministries favored fiscal expansion and were reinforced by foreign governments pressing for greater domestic demand. Appreciation of the mark and yen also tended to favor the expansionists' position. Whether domestic and foreign groups in favor of reflation will now combine efforts and sponsor an international coordination agreement, as in 1978, remains to be seen.
93. Quoting Baker, 'We would prefer not to have to rely on exchange rate adjustments alone to remedy trade imbalances. But clearly, the current U.S. trade deficit cannot be allowed to continue indefinitely. As we have indicated in the past, unless there are additional measures to promote higher growth abroad, there will need to be further exchange rate changes to reduce trade imbalances.' *Washington Post,* 24 September 1986.
94. *Financial Times,* 1, 4, 19, and 22 September 1986.
95. *New York Times,* 7 May 1986.
96. Embassy of Japan, 'Report of the Advisory Group on Economic Structural Adjustment for International Harmony,' and 'Outline of Procedures for the Promotion of Economic Structural Adjustment,' press releases, Washington, D.C., 7 April and 1 May 1986.
97. U.S. Department of the Treasury, press release, Washington, D.C., 31 October 1986.
98. *Wall Street Journal,* 13 January 1987.
99. *IFO-Digest,* 9 (Munich, December 1986): 1–17.
100. *New York Times,* 23 February 1987. Baker reiterated the United States' intention to reach the Gramm-Rudman deficit reduction targets, despite skepticism that this would be done.
101. IMF, *World Economic Outlook,* October 1986; OECD, *Economic Outlook,* 40 (Paris, December 1986).
102. Paul A Volcker, 'Statement before the Committee on Banking, Housing and Urban Affairs, U.S. Senate,' Federal Reserve Board, press release, Washington, D.C., 23 July 1986.
103. Kenneth A. Oye, 'Explaining Cooperation under Anarchy: Hypotheses and Strategies,' *World Politics,* 38 (October 1985): 6.
104. Furthermore, downward rigidity of the real wage in Europe tended to make these governments even more averse to depreciation than they would have been on the grounds of openness alone. During 1984, the general

71

reduction of inflation in Europe helped to explain the greater tendency of European governments to operate monetary policy independently of the United States.

105. This argument is made in Stefano Micossi and Tommaso Padoa-Schioppa, *Can Europeans Control Their Interest Rates?* Centre for European Policy Studies Papers, no. 17 (Brussels, 1984). Greater European unification could substantially alter the financial power differential between Europe and the United States. Cognizant of this, Micossi and Padoa-Schioppa advocate closer monetary cooperation and greater financial liberalization among the countries of the EMS. Indeed, the European Commission, under the leadership of Jacques Delors, successfully promoted such a plan, and agreement was reached in late 1986 to remove an array of capital controls. See, Commission of the European Communities, 'Programme for the Liberalization of Capital Movements in the Community,' press release, Brussels, 23 May 1986; *The Economist,* (22 November 1986): 84.

106. In the same interview in which Mitterrand complained bitterly of Reagan administration intransigence, he acknowledged that his government had underestimated the duration of the world recession and that he should have imposed the March 1983 austerity measures one year earlier. *New York Times,* 11 October 1983.

107. Jeffrey D. Sachs, 'The Dollar and the Policy Mix: 1985,' *Brookings Papers on Economic Activity,* 1:1985: 117–98. To achieve the optimal redistribution of inflation across time, Sachs argues, the United States should have depreciated the dollar earlier. To distinguish between domestic and foreign sources of income and inflation, Marris has designed indexes of 'performance' and 'wellbeing,' in *Deficits and the Dollar,* 51–3.

108. This is consistent with Nau's conclusion for the 1981–83 period, although for different reasons. I agree with Nau that the United States has exercised influence over others' policies through the markets, but believe as well that this stems from the position of the United States in the world economy rather than the particular stance — deflationary or reflationary, free-market or non-market oriented — of U.S. policy.

109. Haas defines consensual knowledge, in turn, as 'a body of beliefs about cause-effect and ends-means relationships among variables (activities, aspirations, values, demands) that is widely accepted by the relevant actors, irrespective of the absolute or final 'truth' of these beliefs.' Cited by Robert L. Rothstein, 'Consensual Knowledge and International Collaboration: Some Lessons from the Commodity Negotiations,' *International Organization,* 38 (Autumn 1984): 736–40.

110. Joseph S. Nye, 'Nuclear Learning and U.S.-Soviet Security Regimes,' paper presented to the American Political Science Association annual meeting, Washington, D.C., 28 August 1986, 11–12.

111. Cohen, 'An Explosion in the Kitchen?' 115–44.

112. James A. Baker, 'Remarks to the 1986 International Monetary Conference, Boston, Massachusetts,' U.S. Department of the Treasury, press release, Washington, D.C., 3 June 1986. The replacement of Regan by Baker as Treasury Secretary is a popular explanation for the subsequent change in U.S. international monetary policy. Their job switch is important in explaining the style and timing of the change in U.S. policy, but the evolution of national interests in foreign reflation and dollar depreciation is the more fundamental explanation. Rather than repudiate his own dollar policy, which was contributing to massive current account deficits and enormous political problems on Capitol Hill, a move to the White House may have looked relatively attractive to Regan. Baker had been privy to a number of meetings at the White House between the President, Regan, and the chairmen of several large American corporations at which the over-

valuation of the dollar was discussed. He was aware of the problem, and might well have calculated that a change in dollar policy would be politically entrepreneurial. Rather than flowing from the change in personnel, the necessity to change foreign economic policy probably contributed to a mutually beneficial job exchange between Regan and Baker in the second Reagan administration.

113. U.S. Office of the President, 'Remarks by the President in Address to the Joint Meeting of the World Bank and International Monetary Fund,' press release, Washington, D.C., 30 September 1986.
114. Differing in its emphasis on the costs of the adjustment, sequence of phases, and motives for changes in foreign policy strategies, the scheme presented here is inspired by a framework developed by Fred Bergsten for interpreting changes in American cooperativeness in both the monetary/ macroeconomic and trade areas. See, 'America's Unilateralism,' in C. Fred Bergsten, Etienne Davignon, and Isamu Miyazaki, *Conditions for Partnership in International Economic Management,* Report to the Trilateral Commission, no. 32 (New York, May 1986), 3–14.
115. Cohen observes that the Carter administration learned more quickly than the Reagan administration about the external consequences of its domestic policies. See, Cohen, 'An Explosion in the Kitchen?'
116. Bergsten, 'America's Unilateralism,' 5–6.
117. Various economic and financial measures might be applied to determine whether the United States current account deficit in 1986 is unsustainable. One common measure is the external debt to GNP ratio, which for the United States is still relatively small and could continue to climb at rates forecast for 1987 — 2–3 percent per year — for several years before even approaching ratios for major Third World debtors. Taking into consideration the fact that the United States borrows largely in its own currency and has a more diversified economy than other large debtors, debt levels themselves do not make the U.S. deficit unsustainable. See, also, Jeffrey A. Frankel, 'The Dazzling Dollar,' and Peter Isard and Lois Stekler, 'U.S. International Capital Flows and the Dollar,' *Brookings Papers on Economic Activity,* 1:1985: 199–217, 219–36.
118. *New York Times,* 10 February 1985.
119. That the outcry in Congress was directed as much toward the administration as it was toward trading partners is illustrated in, I.M. Destler, *American Trade Politics: System Under Stress* (Washington, D.C.: Institute for International Economics, 1986). See, also, 'Protecting Congress or Protecting Trade?,' *Foreign Policy,* 62 (Spring 1986): 96–107.
120. At a chance meeting at Washington, D.C.'s national airport immediately after the Plaza accord, Deputy Treasury Secretary Darman reportedly quipped to Senator Bradley, the author of the Strategic Capital Reserve bill, 'You can take your bill out of the hopper.' *Wall Street Journal,* 9 October 1986. For Congressional reaction to the Plaza accord, see, as well, *Wall Street Journal,* 23 September 1985.
121. Richard N. Cooper, 'External Constraints on European Growth,' paper presented to the Conference on Impediments to European Economic Growth, Brookings Institution, Washington, D.C., 9–10 October 1986. See, also, Stephen D. Cohen, *Uneasy Partnership: Competition and Conflict in U.S.-Japanese Trade Relations* (Cambridge, MA: Ballinger, 1985), chap. 9.
122. Putnam and Henning, *The Bonn Economic Summit Meeting of 1978.*
123. This misconception has crept into the macroeconomic coordination literature as well. See, Michael Stewart, *The Age of Interdependence: Economic Policy in a Shrinking World* (Cambridge, MA: MIT Press, 1984), 75.

124. See, for example, *Financial Times*, 11 September 1986. This lesson was not confined to the Germans, of course. Many Americans faulted the Carter administration for pressing Germany to reflate. Indeed, in 1982, the American Ambassador in Bonn, former Fed Chairman Arthur Burns, admonished the German government for having agreed to the 1978 package! *International Herald Tribune*, 25 February 1982.

125. International political economists formally define a regime as 'sets of implicit or explicit principles, norms, rules, and decision-making procedures around which actor expectations converge in a given area of international relations.' See, Stephen D. Krasner, 'Structural Causes and Regime Consequences: Regimes as Intervening Variables,' *International Organization*, 36 (Spring 1982): 186.

126. See: Keohane, *After Hegemony: Cooperation and Discord in the World Political Economy; International Organization*, 36 (Spring 1982); and Robert O. Keohane and Joseph Nye, *Power and Interdependence* (Boston: Little, Brown, 1977).

127. Nye, 'Nuclear Learning,' especially 24–5. Nye argues that regimes can facilitate learning by providing a focal point around which expectations converge and supplying information that causes people to reassess state interests and perceive cause-effect relationships not previously understood.

128. Williamson, *The Exchange Rate System;* and John Williamson, 'Exchange Rate Management: The Role of Target Zones,' paper presented to the American Economic Association annual meeting, New Orleans, 28–30 December 1986.

129. Ronald I. McKinnon, *An International Standard for Monetary Stabilization*, Policy Analyses in International Economics, no. 3 (Washington, D.C.: Institute for International Economics, March 1984).

130. U.S. House of Representatives, *H.R. 3*, Sec. 405 and 406, 100th Cong., 1st sess., introduced 6 January 1987.

131. Stephen N. Marris, *The Economics and Politics of Managing the World Economy* (Cambridge, MA: MIT Press, forthcoming 1987).

Recent Atlantic Papers

At least four Atlantic Papers are published each year. They may be ordered singly or on a subscription basis. For details of subscription rates and orders for Atlantic Papers prior to No. 62 write to:

The Atlantic Institute for International Affairs
9 Avenue Hoche, 75008 Paris, France
Tel: (1) 42.25.58.17

Atlantic Paper No. 62 and all subsequent papers should be ordered from:
(all orders must be accompanied by payment)

Croom Helm Ltd
Provident House, Burrell Row, Beckenham, Kent BR3 1AT, England
Orders and Enquiries: Tel: (01) 650 6061